C. A. Nelson's
Beauty
AND THE
BEAST

AN ORIGINAL PLAY BY CHELSEA A. NELSON

ISBN-13: 978-1530274000

ISBN-10: 1530274001

CAST of CHARACTERS

Smuk [Smōk] Family

Varakas—a once-wealthy, not quite honest merchant

Hilda—his wife

Gelda—his daughter

Perle— his daughter

Thors—his son

Rubi—his youngest daughter

CASTLE

The Beast—Stevard Sholtze

Knightly—a suit of armor

Goosey—a portrait of a Goose girl

Windy— a Grecian Statue "Lady Admiring Wind" (*so she can be in many poses*)

Jester —a wisecracking face in the wall

Wit—a wisecracking face in the wall

Diana—a bronze statue of Diana, the goddess of the Hunt

GNOMES: Bergen, Leder, Dopple & Ganger (can be 2 gnomes or more)

Eventyr—a painting of a fairy

BANDITS

Gunter—a disgruntled accountant

Frieda—a bandit

Hansel—a musical bandit

Lars—a bandit

Helmut—a bandit

Johanna—a bandit

Pipo—(the pickpocket) (should be the smallest of the group)

Nine, Vadelmar, Jeppe, Bertram, Anders

VILLAGERS

Glena—the Baker

Saffi—Owner of the Wunder Bar

Emil(ia)—her son (or daughter)

Hedda—owner of the Mercantile

Alberte—her sister

Smith—the blacksmith

Rasmus—the postman (if played by a girl, can be named PETRA)

Clara—A seamstress

Anka—her pessimistic cousin

Fritz – the town musician

Author's Note:

I was asked to write an original script for a 2016 Summer Theater Program, and I kept coming back to Beauty and the Beast for many reasons. The classic French tale had already been told by famous film makers for years, but as a girl I had been familiar with the Russian version, where the Beauty had a full family and it turned out that the curse was not incurred by any choice the Beast made, but by his father who had fought with a powerful sorceress. In researching it further, I came to see a theme. The Russian version was really about a marginalized girl and a mistreated boy overcoming the consequences of their parents' bad choices by deciding to make better ones of their own—that struck me.

I set it in Denmark and the German states for a number of reasons: simple costumes, the rules of lordship worked for my story, and I find Germanic languages to be amusing. The German word for "beauty" is "schönheit," but in this version, our Beauty is named Rubi Smuk (pronounced *smoke*), because "smuk" is the Danish word for "beautiful." There are a number of Danish and German comments throughout the play.   Several lines for Eventyr are meant to sound like gibberish, but I have included what she is actually saying; the actress's body language will have to be very clear. It's really funny! Eventyr is frustrated that it comes out the way it does. It shows that she is "fragmented" and unable to form pure sentences until Rubi begins to change the castle.

As all of the CASTLE characters are extensions of EVENTYR, it is ok for each one to be a caricature rather than deeply fleshed out. DIANA is all warrior woman—powerfully feminine. GOOSEY is like a motherly 10-year old taking care of her babies. WINDY is a stereotypical girly girl—flowingly feminine. KNIGHTLY is a true gentleman. JESTER and WIT are just fun!

A note on JESTER and WIT: Faces of jesters wearing hats were carved into beams in dining and entertaining spaces in Germany and Denmark as early as 1400 AD, as a symbol of fun and freedom to speak one's mind. One person may play this part, but it balances the room to have two; they are "one mind." They can be in the walls, the ends of banisters, or similar to carved gargoyles that can move around.

The Dances referred to in the play are German and Danish folk dances. Any type of dance may be used. There is a wide variety of fun folk dances online to draw from.

This play opened July 14, 2016 at Ben Lomond High School in Ogden, Utah for the Ogden School District Summer Theater Program, featuring children from 5 – 17 years old and performed on a proscenium stage.

ACKNOWLEDGEMENTS

Special thanks to the many people who helped me get this script where it is.

Carolyn Stevens, Joyce Wilson and the Ogden School District Board who supported this endeavor.

The Original Cast, who were patient, supportive, talented, and in fact inspired some pretty big changes—especially Zach, Julia, and Ivy.

Ann Washburn, Becky Erkkila, Andrew Brandley, Rozan Holbrook, Sherril Nelson, and Carolee Waddoups for being my unofficial writing circle.

Alpha readers group: Brooke Prothero, Derek Loveland, Jacoba Hurd, Kristina Wilcox, Susan Wilhelm (helped with the German), Sydney Cheshire.

Amberle Stoffers for the creation of a logo that captures the unique elements of the play.

Sarah Gray and her team of students from Yucaipa High School in California who were the second group to perform this script. I thank them for the mistakes/errors they caught and the value they saw.

Thanks to Liam who gave me the idea for the bandits, to River who inspired Eventyr, to Brogan who laughs at all my jokes, and most special thanks to Caleb, who believes in me completely.

ACT 1

SCENE 1: THE SMUK HOUSE

(Scene opens on the inside of a humble house set SR; PERLE, GELDE, THORS, and RUBI are playing a competitive game of charades as HILDE busily goes about homemaking business. VARAKAS has his head bent over papers at his desk but watches his children from time to time as they play. RUBI is up acting out "Hansel and Gretel." Actions include eating a house, being frightened of a witch, showing that THORS is her brother, and should end with dropping breadcrumbs.)

THORS: Planting seeds? Feeding birds?

PERLE: The theme is folk tales, Thors.

THORS: You tell me what folk tale *that* looks like! (*Back to RUBI, who is now indicating her hands.*) Hands? (*RUBI points to her ears*) sounds like... (*She points to her hands*) Hands... (*RUBI nods; his sisters laugh, she looks shy. RUBI takes off her apron, and winds it up, shaping it into a pretzel.*)

THORS: (*Jumping to his feet*) Hansel and Gretel! (*RUBI nods and they celebrate.*)

GELDE: (*Shocked*) How did you guess that?

PERLE: Especially with Rubi's terrible clues.

1

THORS: (*To RUBI*) What were you doing with the—? (*Imitates the throwing out breadcrumbs movement she used.*)

RUBI: I was laying down a trail of breadcrumbs.

GELDE: You're still losing. And now it's our turn.

THORS: (*Taunting*) To lose?

GELDE: (*Dryly*) Ha ha.

> (*THORS and RUBI confer and they write something on a piece of paper. RUBI looks confused, but THORS is laughing. He hands the paper to PERLE.*)

THORS: Here you go, Perle. Gelde will never guess this one!

> (*PERLE reads the paper and makes a face, first at the paper and then at THORS, upset and questioning. THORS, pleased with himself, leans back in his seat.*)

THORS: Just do your best, Perle.

> (*PERLE begins acting out the clue: "The Beastly King." She tries contorting her body into a beast, making fangs, growling, hunching over. She makes fingers on her head to indicate a crown.*)

GELDE: (*Guessing*) Animal? Wild animal. Hunchback? Hunchback of Notre Dame? Baba Yaga? How many words is it? (*PERLE indicates three*) Three... Um... The Fox and the Hare? A moose? A rabid queen? A Moose queen?

PERLE: Ugh! I give up!!

GELDE: What was it?

PERLE: The Beastly King. (*To THORS*) What is that?

THORS: You could have acted out a king trapping a fairy!

GELDE: What good would that have done?

PERLE: It doesn't count! Mama! Tell him it doesn't count.

GELDE: It's not fair if we don't know the story in the first place.

HILDA: Stop your whining! You know the story well enough, Gelde. I told it to you many times when you were young.

GELDE: (*Haughty*) Well, I don't remember.

THORS: Yes you do. Once upon a time, the steward of a fine castle saved a fairy in the forest, and she granted him a wish.

PERLE: What was the wish?

HILDA: (*Interjecting*) To have all that the wealth and power of a king, but never have to work for it.

THORS: My kind of wish!

HILDA: (*Glaring*) How like your father you are. (*Sits down to engage and tell the story*) But you can't get something for nothing, my children. The steward gave no thought to the cost, until his first child was born.

RUBI: (*Aghast*) What happened then, Mama?

HILDA: The baby was born a monster!

CHILDREN: (*Gasp!*)

HILDA: When the man saw the cost of his reckless wish, well, you'd think he would change his tune. (*At VARAKAS*) Try to reverse it, perhaps, to spare his wife and save his child. But no, the man simply grew more and more wealthy. Eventually, he became king. He took his wife and cursed child to live in a castle enchanted to fulfill his every wish and he set about ruling the people.

THORS: (*Laughing*) But he was terrible! The servants all left, the castle fell apart. He just griped and complained. The *kingdom* even began to fail, and his wife died of shame!

HILDA: Didn't have to work, so he forgot how to appreciate things. (*Pointedly*) Remind you of anyone?

VARAKAS: (*Teasing*) Not anyone I know.

PERLE: Then what happened?

HILDA: When the fairy heard what a terrible ruler this man had become, she offered to release his son from the curse if he would give up the kingdom and let a wiser man rule.

THORS: (*Interrupting, dramatic*) But he wouldn't! He captured the fairy and locked her in an enchanted cage that drained her magic and made her weak. Then the Beastly King died alone and miserable, leaving both the fairy and the son trapped in the castle he could not take with him. (*Sits back, satisfied.*)

PERLE: That's awful.

RUBI: I don't like that story.

GELDE: Of course you don't, Rubi. There is no happy ending.

HILDA: What did you expect? This is Denmark, not France. Our tales end as they end—happy or no.

PERLE: A dreary story to go with our dreary game and this dreary house.

HILDA: Come, come, my children. It is a roof isn't it? It has four walls, doesn't it? Be grateful for what you have—even the tale to entertain you.

VARAKAS: (To HILDA) I seem to remember it was your favorite, once.

HILDA: Not anymore, Varakas.

PERLE: Why not Mama?

> (*HILDA pauses.*)

RUBI: Because, Perle, the Beastly king never changes.

4

VARAKAS: My girls like to believe that people can change, is that it?

HILDA: (*Snorting*) In fairy tales.

RUBI: People can change in real life, too, Mama.

HILDA: For the worse, in my experience.

VARAKAS: (*Crosses to her*) Silence your sour wind, my dear, before you spoil the fruit (*indicating the children*).

HILDA: (*Strong*) I am not the one who risked our livelihood! You used to be a respectable businessman.

VARAKAS: I still am!

HILDA: Bah! I warned you, and yet you invest with that snake, Gunter Rask, and lump all your trade goods onto three ships as a front to lure other traders, but whose goods were lost at sea? OURS! Sailing from *Aarhus* to Lisbon in *March*? Who ever heard of such a thing?!

VARAKAS: That is why we were able to sell it to the desperate, my dear.

HILDA: Your speculation lost us everything. You have taken us from a prosperous life in the city to one of—

GELDA/PERLE: Suffering!

HILDA: I was going to say poverty.

VARAKAS: Now, Hilda. No one could have known—

HILDA: I knew! You said you would give up the con, Varakas; be honest! The business was thriving before you took this risk, going back to your old ways.

VARAKAS: Those old ways are what got us started. And I seem to remember a very beautiful young woman who found the danger of a well run confidence quite attractive back in the day.

HILDA: (*Half-smiles*) Not anymore. (*He tickles her neck; she smacks his hand.*) You cannot turn my head, you nincompoop. (*VARAKAS nuzzles up close to her, causing her to giggle; VARAKAS, satisfied he has gotten himself out of hot water, goes back to his desk*).

RUBI: It is not so bad here, is it mother? I rather like the country.

HILDA: Mark me, Rubi. I do not complain of the life. I would just rather your father be a contented, honest man. (*Looks around, satisfied*) No, this life does not bother me.

RUBI: Me neither.

PERLE: (*Rolls her eyes*) Oh, please!

THORS: (*Dramatically*) I'm bored.

VARAKAS: (*Sighing and sitting down*) Besides, my strudel, we don't even know what happened to the ships. "Location unknown" isn't actually lost...it's still enough to hope.

PERLE: But not enough to trade on.

GELDA: We haven't any credit left anywhere.

HILDA: Well, the three of you spent on the name of Varakas and Hilda Smuk for all it was worth, that's certain.

GELDA: Now it's worth nothing.

THORS: (*Clarifying*) Less than nothing, actually.

RUBI: (*Hand on Papa's shoulder*) You and your name are still prized possessions to me, Papa.

PERLE: (*Disgusted*) Ugh! Mama, make her stop!

HILDA: That reminds me, you have a letter, Varakas. (*She produces a letter and hands it to RUBI who hands it to VARAKAS.*)

VARAKAS: (*Confused*) I thought no one knew we were here. (*Opens the letter and begins reading.*)

6

GELDE: (*Whispering to THORS*) What did you gamble away this time?

THORS: Me?! (*Accusingly*) Where did that shawl come from? (*Stick out tongues at each other.*)

VARAKAS: (*Jumps out of his seat, whooping and startling the whole room*) Ah ha! I knew it! I could feel it in my lucky bones!

ALL: What is it? What news? What has happened? Etc.

VARAKAS: One of the ships is safe and returning to port. The ice is too thick for it to reach *Aarhus*, so it will dock in Hamburg. Gunter requests that I come meet it and...settle the remaining debts and loans. Hmmm...that might get slippery. Gunter assures me there is plenty in the hold! (*To HILDA*) I told you! He is a good, trusting fellow!

HILDA: (*Snorts*) But is he trust *worthy*? (*Shakes her head*) This will bite you one day...

PERLE: You must set off at once!

THORS: I'll ready the horse and cart!

GELDE: It's our only horse, Thors!

THORS: (*Dismissively*) Then *you* can pull the cart. Besides, we will have the money to buy twelve when Papa returns.

VARAKAS: Indeed we will, my son (*Slapping him on the back*). Rubi, get my coat. I'm off for Germany posthaste! (*HILDA exits.*) Now, what shall I bring back for my patient, longsuffering children?

GELDE: A golden necklace set with fire-stones, and strings of pearls!

PERLE: A silver mirror, and brush, and diamond combs for my hair!

THORS: A sword and the finest leather boots!

HILDA: (*Entering*) Bring them something useful. I need more pots.

VARAKAS: Not after this, *Min kaere*! We will have servants again, and a cook! *You* will not have to lift a finger.

HILDA: I don't mind lifting a finger in honest work, Varakas. Pots. And a wooden spoon; I have a feeling I'll be needing another.

VARAKAS: What's the matter with that one?

HILDA: (*Menacingly*) I'll be breaking it over your backside if you come home a dishonest disgrace.

VARAKAS: (*Swallows*) I shall be on my best behavior, my succulent honey crumble.

HILDA: Mmm hmmm. (*She offers her cheek and he kisses it.*)

RUBI: (*Coming up to them*) Here, take this scarf to keep warm. I made it for you.

VARAKAS: You have had no new supplies in ages, Rubi. How—?

RUBI: I took the yarn from a sweater Thors outgrew, and made this of it.

HILDA: Our daughter can make sense out of chaos, Varakas.

VARAKAS: (*Turns to quiet RUBI*) And what shall I bring back for you, my darling?

RUBI: (*Looking around the shabby house, concerned*) A knapweed, Papa.

VARAKAS: The flower of Germany?

RUBI: I've never seen one.

VARAKAS: Is that all? It's a rather plain gift. (*RUBI nods tenderly.*) Well then, if my beauty desires a blue knapweed to compare with our red clover of Denmark, I shall bring it. (*Kisses her on the fore-head. Family loads him up with all his supplies and VARAKAS exits*)

ALL: *Hej Hej, Favel, and God rejse!*

8

SCENE 2: GUNTER'S OFFICE IN HAMBURG

(GUNTER is seated at a table and Center Left with maps as well as a bag of money to show the room as a shipping office. BANDITS are behind the table gambling their time and money. VARAKAS enters DSL. FREIDA stops him.)

FREIDA: Herr Rask has been waiting for you.

VARAKAS: I'm sure he has! I came as soon as I could. Thank you, good fellow!

FREIDA: I'm a woman.

VARAKAS: And a charming one at that.

FREIDA: Just go inside.

VARAKAS: (*Entering the room with bravado*) Gunter, my old friend!

GUNTER: (*Doubtful*) Am I?

VARAKAS: What kind of a question is that? Of course you are!

GUNTER: Friends normally leave a forwarding address, Varakas.

VARAKAS: It was not my choice, Gunter. My wife ran up monumental debts, and with the ships missing, we had no choice but to flee the creditors.

GUNTER: *And* your partners?

VARAKAS: I would not have left you wondering. But, you know the old saying: When the wife says "Move," you move the world.

GUNTER: I have never heard that.

VARAKAS: Really? (*Nervous*) Ah. Well, it is French. (*Laughs nervously, then acts sad*) I had to go, Gunter. I trusted that with you here, there was no need to worry.

GUNTER: Then no doubt, you will be pleased with how I have settled affairs here in your absence.

VARAKAS: I am sure I will be. What's left?

GUNTER: Your debts were indeed substantial. The royal navy sent out a notice of your ship's arrival, and your creditors were faster getting here than you were.

VARAKAS: (*Proven*) I told you—

GUNTER: Here is all that remains to split between us. (*Hands VARAKAS a purse not quite filled with coins and gulden bills.*)

VARAKAS: Ah, yes, 20/80 wasn't that it?

GUNTER: 50/50 I believe was the agreed upon split.

VARAKAS: (*Crossing behind GUNTER'S table to read the contract*) Really? Are you certain?

GUNTER: (*Not pleased; slaps the papers on the desk firmly*) Very.

VARAKAS: Well, then you are probably right. (*Makes a show of counting the money in the bag*) Oh, but we need smaller papers; it is not even. I'll head to the purser and have it changed to *krone* for me and *gulden* for you, my friend. Then we can go for a drink! Yes? Alright. (*Begins to exit to the door.*)

GUNTER: (*Stopping him*) I'll be waiting for you, Varakas.

FREIDA: We all will. (*Other bandits stand behind GUNTER*)

VARAKAS: I'll not be long. (*Exits, quickly*)

FREIDA: (*To GUNTER*) You think he's coming back?

GUNTER: (*Shakes his head*) But give him twenty minutes. I would like to be surprised.

HANSEL: And if he doesn't return?

GUNTER: You know what to do.

FREIDA: (*Menacing*) Yes, we do.

Hansel: (*Jovially; to the tune of "Wassailing"*) Oh! Here we go a-thiever-ing among the trees so green, Here we go a-thiever-ing, our money to be seen, we'll attack and we'll steal, and we'll make that con man squeal—

GUNTER: (*Smacks HANSEL upside the head*) What did I tell you?!

HANSEL: But we're the *Singing Bandits*!

FREIDA: That name was never agreed upon.

GUNTER: (*Stammering with frustration*) Just...Just...Just...follow him to the woods well out of town, and get me my money.

FREIDA: Ja!

GUNTER: And to teach him a lesson, get all of it. I want every *gulden* and *krone* that man has.

BANDITS: Ja, Ja! (*Or make up a humorous musical salute.*)

    (*Lights out as they Exit.*)

SCENE 3: A FOREST

(Varakas Enters front of curtain and we hear forest sounds; wind etc; he appears hurried and worried. He hears the BANDITS to the tune of "What do you do with a Drunken Sailor.")

HANSEL: (*Singing*) What do you do with a dirty con man?

LARS: (*Singing*) What do you do with a dirty con man?

HELMUT: (*Singing*) What do you do with a dirty con man walking through a forest...?

(*VARAKAS comes face to face with FREIDA.*)

FREIDA: (*Smiling*) We rob him.

> *(VARAKAS attempts to escape, but the BANDITS surround, beat, and rob him. BANDITS exit Right, singing:)*

BANDITS: (*To the tune of B-I-N-G-O*) There was a con man ran a con, and crossed our noble boss-man.

HANSEL: (*Singing*) Now we've got the loot,

LARS: (*Singing*) Don't forget his boots,

HELMUT: (*Singing*) Leave him in the woods and ... and ... (*stumped, he looks to each until FREIDA walks through them, all business*)

FREIDA: (*Singing*) And Bingo was his name-o! (*BANDITS Exit, laughing.*)

> *(VARAKAS stands and limps LEFT, falling half on, half off stage. Someone drags him offstage. Lights out.)*

SCENE 4: THE CASTLE

(Lights up on the interior of a German castle. Most of the stage is still shadowed, with the suggestion of people standing about. A large banquet table is spread with food the GNOMES underneath; a pedestal table and chairs are tipped over and other loose bits of furniture are scattered about the space. It's a mess. VARAKAS is lying on a chaise DL near the fireplace. Audience should not be able to see the CASTLE clearly yet. They are simply voices coming from the dark.)

DIANA: (*Firmly*) It's not possible.

GOOSEY: He did, I tell you! Master brought the man in from the woods.

EVENTYR: Gramshtuckle for horsenfiven an kellock! (*He really did, I can't believe it!*)

JESTER: (*Yawning*) If I didn't see it, it didn't happen.

DIANA: He's right there you boulder-head. How do you think he got in here?

KNIGHTLY: Must have been the Master, since none of us can leave the boundaries of the castle grounds...

WINDY: (*Despairing*) I can't even leave this room!

WIT: I can't even leave this wall.

KNIGHTLY: But the Master caring for someone?

GOOSEY: He had Bergen and Leder bandage him!

DIANA: That sounds nothing like the Master at all—

GOOSEY: (*Fondly*) If you ask me, it's just like him, really.

DIANA: Will you stop with that? He is not the tender little baby you think he is!

KNIGHTLY: All of you, quiet! I think he's waking up...

> *(CASTLE shushes each other until VARAKAS is awake;*
> *then they are silent. VARAKAS feels a bandage under*
> *his shirt. Confused and dazed, he looks around at the*
> *dirty, run down castle. He stands and wanders about*
> *the room. He inspects the fire, WINDY who is USL, and*
> *across the room to DIANA who is posed near the*
> *tipped pedestal table. VARAKAS goes to the banquet*
> *table. The table spread with fine foods seems out of*
> *place.)*

VARAKAS: Hello? (*There is no answer. He goes towards the food, smelling it. It smells fine. He checks over his shoulder and begins eating. CASTLE begins whispering, but the audience cannot understand them. He hears whispers and shushing. He is uneasy, but hungry. He sits on the nearest chair; it breaks from under him. He backs away from the mess and runs into the banister, breaking it. The silence makes him uncomfortable. VARAKAS swallows and decides to leave. He loads his pockets with food and as he turns to leave he sees a blue scarf embroidered with*) A knapweed for Rubi. (*He considers, and then shoves it in his satchel.*)

BEAST: (*Ominously, from the stairs USL*) Was it not enough?

VARAKAS: (*Startled*) Who is there?

BEAST: Help, healing, and food are not enough?

VARAKAS: (*Louder, bold with fear*) Who is there?

> *(BEAST jumps over the railing and bounds to the ta-*
> *ble, a large cloak making him appear ten feet tall.*
> *VARAKAS, terrified, shouts and cowers.)*

VARAKAS: Don't hurt me!

BEAST: (*Sounding like he wants to hurt him*) I do not intend to hurt you.

VARAKAS: I didn't know anyone was here!

BEAST: (*Indicating the food and room*) Where did you think all of this came from?

VARAKAS: I wasn't thinking!

BEAST: (*Pacing on the table*) Obviously. What were you doing in the woods? (*Absently kicking things off as he goes; gnomes quickly retrieve what falls, which startles VARAKAS.*)

VARAKAS: (*Lying to gain sympathy*) My wife died this past year. I have been working in Hamburg while my children stay with family. I finally earned enough to bring them home and was on my way there when I was robbed by bandits.

BEAST: (*Pause*) I had your wounds bandaged.

VARAKAS: Thank you.

BEAST: Yet you have stolen from me.

VARAKAS: Just a scarf...

BEAST: (*Loudly, banging the table like an angry gorilla*) MY scarf!

VARAKAS: (*Startled*) I'm sorry, it was a gift for my youngest daughter. She likes flowers.

BEAST: (*Confused*) A scarf is not a flower.

VARAKAS: Yes, but it has the flower on it that—

BEAST: (*Interrupting him*) You have broken my belongings. What have you to say on that count?

VARAKAS: (*Defensive*) I was dizzy—

BEAST: Someone shall have to repair these damages. (*The CASTLE murmurs*) Someone who can go from room to room (*CASTLE still murmurs—he shouts at them*) Someone who knows how! (*They fall silent. To VARAKAS*) You must stay and repair my castle.

VARAKAS: I cannot! I *must* go to my children. They will starve if I never return. (*Has to up the ante*) Please sir, my youngest will surely die without the proper medicines. I have disappointed them in every way.

BEAST: (*Jumps down from the table, barely missing VARAKAS; Bitterly*) This is the wrong place to seek mercy.

>   (*CASTLE murmurs soothingly.*)

BEAST: (*Pacing away; reasonably*) I know I could. I suppose that— (*shouting*) It's MY castle isn't' it?! (*CASTLE falls silent; Eventyr plays soft music.*)

VARAKAS: (*Playing humble*) Sir? My children.

BEAST: (*Suddenly*) You may take all of that (*indicating a trunk and two bags spilling with wealth*) for your family. It's easily enough to support them for years.

VARAKAS: Oh, bless you, sir!

BEAST: (*Backing away*) But, you must promise to come back and work for me until the debt is paid.

VARAKAS: (*Looking at the wealth*) Even a tenth of that...it would take forever to repay!

BEAST: (*With finality*) Then forever it is.

VARAKAS: What if I should refuse?

>   (*Quietly growling; BEAST going closer to VARAKAS. He
>   steps into the light, and VARAKAS can finally see he is*

a beast, a monster. BEAST sniffs VARAKAS menacingly.)

BEAST: I will be able to find you—and your family—wherever you go.

VARAKAS: (*Terrified, and sees that agreeing is the only way he'll survive.*) I give you my word; I will return in three days to repay the debt.

BEAST: (*Grunts. BEAST haphazardly loads Varakas with gold and bags and jewels. VARAKAS turns to leave.*) In three days!

VARAKAS: I am a man of my word. (*He stumbles out, laden with the treasures.*)

BEAST: We shall see.

    (Lights out.)

SCENE 5: THE SMUK HOUSE

(Lights up on the interior of the Smuk House. VARA-KAS is ill, resting on a chaise where his desk used to be. RUBI is reading near him.)

VARAKAS: *(Wakes up, groggy.)* Where am I?

RUBI: You are home, Papa; just rest.

VARAKAS: How long?

RUBI: You have been asleep for nearly two days.

VARAKAS: *(Worried)* The gold?

RUBI: Be calm, Papa. We have it and everything is good now.

VARAKAS: No. No it isn't.

RUBI: What?

VARAKAS: *(Faintly)* I have made a huge mistake, Rubi. We have to leave. Call everyone. I need to speak to everyone.

RUBI: Mama! Perle, Gelde, Thors!

> *(They ALL enter, well dressed and happy.)*

HILDA: You are awake! I cannot believe all this, my love. You did well. *(Kisses him on the head)*.

GELDE/PERLE/THORS: Oh thank you Papa! We always knew you were the best. Don't I look wonderful, etc.

VARAKAS: Quiet, all of you! *(They fall silent)* I was robbed in the woods on the road from Hamburg.

HILDA: *(Worried)* What?

THORS: Then where did all this—?

VARAKAS: I was helped by a (*he decides to edit*) wealthy man living in the forest, who heard my troubles and offered me a loan.

PERLE: Oh, good job, father.

GELDE: How wise you are!

HILDA: (*Concerned*) And what did that cost you, my dear?

VARAKAS: I had to promise to go back and work off the debt.

(*ALL gasp and look at the pile of wealth.*)

HILDA: Oh, Varakas, but all this? How long...?

VARAKAS: (*Sadly*) I believe the word he used was "forever."

(*BEAT*)

PERLE: Ha!

THORS: The joke's on him, right Father?

GELDE: (*Laughing*) Good one, Papa!

VARAKAS: Children, quiet! I made the deal, and honestly, I didn't intend to go back.

HILDA: No surprise.

VARAKAS: But he threatened to find and kill us if I don't. All of us.

(*THORS, GELDE, PERLE pause, then wail.*)

HILDA: Bite your tongues before I smack them out of your heads! (*They go silent instantly. HILDA X's to VARAKAS, softer*) Do you believe he would? (*VARAKAS nods*) Then you must go. This is not the same as others you've swindled.

VARAKAS: But it is forever! Who will provide for you?

HILDA: There will be no need for providing if we are dead.

VARAKAS: I cannot believe he could find us, though. (*Doubting his own words*) We can simply disappear as before. We have enough to run, Hilda. We could go to Belgium as we have always dreamed!

RUBI: (*Ashamed*) Oh, Father.

VARAKAS: (*Sadly*) Don't look at me like that.

RUBI: You promised. Does your word mean nothing?

VARAKAS: It's not as simple as that.

RUBI: Yes, it is. (*Stands; firmly*) I'll go.

HILDA: No, Rubi! This is your father's mess.

RUBI: Even if Father were willing, he is too sick to make the trip, and too old for hard labor.

HILDA: Well, that is true...You are not a young man anymore, Varakas.

VARAKAS: (*Pleading*) *No one* has to go! I am sure it will work itself out!

RUBI: All we have is our honor. I do not know about the rest of you, but I want to keep it.

HILDA: You are not alone, my precious Rubi. But you are too young to sign away your life. I will go.

GELDE: Mama! No! Who will cook and clean. You know I am no good at that.

PERLE: And who would care for Papa?

THORS: Or care for me?

HILDA: (*Looking at VARAKAS*) I suppose I cannot leave him like this. But one of us shall have to go.

GELDE: Just send Rubi.

PERLE: She already volunteered! And Rubi doesn't mind hard work. She's so *honorable* like that.

THORS: We won't miss her around here, not really. Any of us could do what she does.

RUBI: Thors is right. He can manage here. And Gelde and Perle, they have suitors and friends. I can go; it feels like I must.

HILDA: (*Turns to RUBI*) Forever is a big word. I don't know what you can do for this man and his fine house. You are not strong or talented or especially clever. Well, you are a good girl. That is something. And what do I always say?

RUBI: Something is better than nothing.

HILDA: (*To PERLE, GELDE, and THORS*) Go pack for your sister. (*Hugs RUBI, at a loss for words; offers her the shawl from her own shoulders.*) Of all my children, you will likely survive the best in this life because you see beauty wherever you are.

> (*The CHILDREN return.*)

RUBI: I will make you proud, Mama.

HILDA: Make yourself proud, my girl.

RUBI: (*Nods. She turns to leave, but, emotional, turns back*). I will be a woman of my word. (*Squares her shoulders and Exits.*)

SCENE 5A: A FOREST

(Front of curtain; the BANDITS are dancing in a circle near a campfire, singing to the tune of "Heigh-Ho the Derry-O.")

HANSEL: (*Singing*) A-thieving we will go, a-thieving we will go!

ALL: Hei-Ho the Derry-o a-thieving we will go.

PEPO: (*Singing*) The bandit takes the gold, the bandit takes the gold!

ALL: Hei-Ho the Derry-o, the bandit takes the gold.

LARS: (*Singing*) The victim wails and moans, the victim wails and moans!

ALL: Hei-Ho, the Derry-O the victim wails and moans.

JOHANA: (*Singing*) The bandits run amok, the bandits run amok.

ALL: Hei-Ho, the Derry-o the bandits run Amok!

FREIDA: (*Singing*) And when we've taken all, away the victims crawl.

ALL: Hei-Ho, the Derry-o, we'll have ourselves a ball! Hey!

> *(All Laugh. RUBI enters SR searching for the path her father described.)*

RUBI: Excuse me.

LARS: (*Defensive*) Who goes there!

RUBI: I am looking for the path through the woods. The villagers told me there was a grand house out this way.

FREIDA: (*Scoffing*) A pile of rubble, more like.

HELMUT: Didn't anyone tell you the story?

RUBI: What story?

HANSEL: Oh, it's a tale as old as time!

RUBI: (*Shakes her head*) No.

NINE: People say it's cursed; that there's a monster, and that the wood is haunted by ghosts.

LARS: No, it's a dragon! It sleeps on piles of gold and can only be killed if its shot by an arrow through a hole is its armored skin!

HANSEL: You're thinking of a different story, Lars.

LARS: Am I?

RUBI: My father has been there. I am going to work for the master of the house.

FREIDA: Well don't say we didn't warn you. (*Circles RUBI, attempting to distract her while PIPO picks her pocket*) These woods are danger-ous. For wealthy folk such as (*PIPO shakes his head, she has no purse or jewelry*) someone else. Get out of here. Why are you bothering us? The path is that way!

RUBI: That way?

ANDERS: Yeah, down the dell.

HANSEL: The path is straight; you can see it well!

LARS: But who knows what may be

ALL: (*Singing*) Lurking on the journey!

FREIDA: (*Smacking them*) Will you two shut up? You'll steal anything. (*to RUBI*) Just get outta here, ya peasant. Git.

HANSEL: Yeah, thataway!

RUBI: (*Hurrying off*) *Mange tak.*

LARS: (*Frightened*) You really think there is a monster there?

FREIDA: (*Eyes her companion before shouting*) NO!

(*Lights out.*)

SCENE 6: THE CASTLE

(RUBI enters through doors UC. The doors should be difficult to open or hanging on a hinge. She walks in, over things, and sees the table spread with good food. This time there is a fire lit in the fireplace.)

RUBI: (*Nervous; walks around the room, sees no sign of a person so calls out*) Hello?

BEAST: (*From the top of the stairs SR*) Who are you?

RUBI: (*Frightened*) Rubi.

BEAST: How did you find this place?

RUBI: My father (*produces a letter*). I have this letter from him (*going towards BEAST who motions for her to stay where she is. She backs up.*) My name is Rubi. I have come in place of Varakas Smuk. I am here to work off his debt.

BEAST: (*Scoffing*) You?

RUBI: My father was ill when he returned. (*Swallows*) I am young. I can work.

BEAST: (*Crosses the space to top of stairs SL, surveying her*) You are tiny.

RUBI: (*Looking herself over; unsure how to answer*) Thank you?

BEAST: You cannot possibly repay the debt. (*Angry*) That scoundrel tricked me!

RUBI: (*Going towards the shadow of him on the stairs*) No! Well; yes, and no. My father *is* very ill. And I *can* work.

BEAST: But?

RUBI: Let's just leave it at that.

24

BEAST: (*Looking her over*) I need a servant who can fix my castle; repair what your father broke!

RUBI: (*Glancing around the mess*) Surely, he didn't do *all* of this?

BEAST: (*Growling*)

RUBI: (*Confused*) I do not mean to offend you. You supplied my family with great wealth. But my father...could not repay it.

BEAST: So you volunteered to come in his place?

RUBI: Yes

BEAST: Why?

RUBI: (*Embarrassed*) I was the least needed at home.

BEAST: I knew it. I needed a workhorse and they sent me a show pony.

RUBI: (*Indignant*) I am more than a pretty face. I can and will do whatever is required to repay the debt.

(*The BEAST scurries towards her, the movement odd and animalistic.*)

BEAST: Will you marry me?

RUBI: (*Frightened*) No.

BEAST: (*Sadly, turning away*) So...not *anything*, then.

RUBI: (*Embarrassed*) Anything within reason.

BEAST: (*Bitterly*) Within reason...

(*BEAT*)

RUBI: When should I start?

BEAST: Now.

RUBI: Where is the kitchen? I will prepare dinner for you.

BEAST: No. Take care of the castle and leave me alone.

RUBI: But—

BEAST: You will soon learn that the castle deserves more attention than I do. Your tasks are on the table. (*He Exits.*)

RUBI: (*Picks up a large scroll that rolls down and across the stage. Surprised, she laughs*) Oh, is this all? (*The BEAST is gone. Calls out*) I will do it and more! You'll see! (*Looking around the room; a little overwhelmed*) After all, I have forever.

SCENE 7: THE CASTLE

(This scene is a series of Vignettes, backed by music and marked with changing lights, as well as improvements to the set to show the passage of time. BERGEN and LEDER can scramble behind her or hide throughout the set as the scenes go, as the director chooses. The vignettes may change to fit the set designed, but the growth of RUBI must follow these examples.)

Vignette 1: Dusting

(RUBI is dusting, and trying to hide a crack in the wall above the fireplace. BEAST enters from Stage right, taking off his cloak, spraying dust (baby powder) in her face as he exits, disrupting the vase of flowers she just put up. She catches it; sneezes.)

GOOSEY: Gesundheit.

(RUBI turns but no one is there, suspicious, RUBI exits. CASTLE glare at Goosey.)

(Light Change.)

Vignette 2: Scrubbing

(RUBI is scrubbing the floor. BEAST walks across it without noticing her or her work. She just sighs, resigned, and scrubs harder.)

(Light Change.)

Vignette 3: Moving

(RUBI is attempting to move the large chaise from SL to SR; it is hard work to do alone. She tries pushing, but slips and lands on it, face first. Then tries pulling it

and accidentally pulls the dirty blanket off, falling on her butt, covered in dust. She sits and cries.)

(Light Change.)

Vignette 4: Fixing

(RUBI is fixing the banister her father broke. Triumphant, she has a moment of celebration to herself. CASTLE rejoices silently, but freeze when RUBI turns.)

(Light Change.)

Vignette 5: RUBI meets the CASTLE

(RUBI enters SR carrying firewood, dropping sticks as she exits LEFT. GNOMES enter and pick them up, following her off. RUBI screams and runs back onstage from LEFT, falling over herself as GNOMES chase her, apologetically.)

DIANA: *(Jumping to RUBI's aid with sword drawn)* I am at your side!

(RUBI screams and backs away, falling into KNIGHTLY's arms.)

WINDY: *(To DIANA)* Put that down, you will frighten her!

KNIGHTLY: Careful, my lady.

(RUBI faints and KNIGHTLY, DIANA and GNOMES carry her to the chaise).

GOOSEY: Be careful with her, Knightly!

KNIGHTLY: I know no other way to be, my dear Goosey.

DIANA: You know how to be pompous.

WINDY: Give the poor dear some air *(Shooing away the GNOMES)*. She needs air.

WIT: You'd know all about hot air, Windy! *(Laughs at his bad joke)*.

28

WINDY: (*Rolls her eyes*) Do you never tire of the same jokes, Jester? (*Dramatically*) You've mocked my name for simply ever!

WIT: There's nothing better to do.

JESTER: We haven't had any other excitement in (*mocking her voice*) *simply ever.*

GOOSEY: I'm just glad we have each other. (*They all moan*) No, really! I know I say it all the time, but this existence would be downright drab without each and every one of you.

EVENTYR: (*Disbelief at the conversation*) A worden jolleyfall there being for whereat the palactalic landwind be fon-rondenfen! (*Absolutely! I don't know if you've noticed, but we are the perfect balance of every personality.*)

GOOSEY: Exactly, Eventyr.

WINDY: Did you understand her that time?

GOOSEY: No, but I'm sure it makes her feel better to think that I did.

DIANA: Just throw some water on her.

(*GNOMES run off stage.*)

KNIGHTLY: (*Shocked and gallant*) I cannot do harm or surprise to a young lady!

DIANA: Then you better not let her see your face.

JESTER: (*Brashly*) Bullseye!

WIT: Point to Diana!

WINDY: (*Turning on them*) Now all of you, just let the girl be—

(*GNOMES return; BERGEN has a small glass of water tosses it in RUBI's face. She wakes spluttering. Everyone freezes, including the GNOMES, though freezing proves they are the ones who threw the water. RUBI squeals and pulls away from them, then comes close to them to check if they are stone. She tweaks LEDER's nose.)*

LEDER: (*Screams*) Ah!

(BERGEN, DOPPLE, and GANGER *scream; they ALL run around in a small circle, wailing.*)

GOOSEY: Do stop that. You'll frighten her!

EVENTYR: (*Frustrated*) Whart givrimlich por oven stop canwick flamgorb!! *(You can't control those little monsters!)*

RUBI: (*In awe*) I'm dreaming. I'm not awake. I fell and hit my head.

KNIGHTLY: (*Leaning over to face her*) Do you really think I'm dreamy?

RUBI: (*Beat, then shouts in his face*) WHAT IS HAPPENING?! *(KNIGHTLY stumbles back, breaking the banister RUBI just repaired. She rushes over.)* Oh! I just fixed that!

GOOSEY: We know!

WINDY: We saw you.

KNIGHTLY: A thousand apologies, my lady.

RUBI: You are forgiven, sir knight. Wait, you saw me? Then you have been here all along?

DIANA: (*Snappy*) Where else would we be?

RUBI: (*Confused*) I...uh.

WINDY: (*Laughing*) Let's not be rude, Diana. (*To RUBI*) Don't mind her if she's a little curt. Goddess of the Hunt and all.

EVENTYR: (*Politely*) For offendom withersoever a gimlet of rivenlight, salive' up on the catterwall and fishenroad. *(Her tongue may be as sharp as her sword, but she will defend her friends to the bitter end.)*

RUBI: I beg your pardon?

30

EVENTYR: (*Yelling, slowly*) For offendom withersoever a gimlet of rivenlight, salive' up on the catterwall and fishenroad. (*Quietly, to herself*) Gonewithenstop grablem a pompie quall. (*I get so tired of no one understanding me when I say awesome things!*) (*Hits the side of her painting.*)

(*RUBI looks to the others for clarification.*)

WINDY: Aaannd, that's Eventyr. (*Explanatory*) She's a painting. (*WINDY attempts to make sense of it.*) She's Gaulish, so she speaks Gaul-ish...we think.

RUBI: Oh. What did she say?

KNIGHTLY: Who ever knows?

WIT: Who cares?

EVENTYR: (*Menacing*) Brandyfitstercoal, sharpy. (*Just wait until I get out of this painting!*)

WINDY: (*Grandly, striking a pose*) I am "Lady Admiring Wind." You may call me Windy. I was chiseled by a Great Artist in the fourteenth century.

DIANA: So she says...

GOOSEY: Diana, don't be jealous simply because Windy is made of marble.

DIANA: I'm not jealous of *her*!

GOOSEY: Bronze may tarnish, but you are just as lovely.

DIANA: (*Embarrassed*) Goosey!

GOOSEY: Forgive me. (*To RUBI*) I am The Goose Girl, and you may call me Gloriana Venezuela Jim Dandy.

RUBI: What an...extraordinary name.

JESTER: Don't call her that. It only encourages her.

31

KNIGHTLY: (*On his feet and bowing with a flourish*) We address her as Goosey. I am Knightly, at your service, my lady. (*Attempts to kiss her hand.*)

RUBI: Pleased to meet you. (*To BERGEN, LEDER, DOPPLE and GANG-ER*) And who are these little, uh...

KNIGHTLY: These are the Master's chefs.

BERGEN: Bergen.

LEDER: Leder.

DOPPLE: Dopple.

GANGER: Ganger!

KNIGHTLY: They are Tomtes

RUBI: They're what?

WIT: Glorified German Gnomes is all!

JESTER: What about us?!

KNIGHTLY: And that's Wit and Jester.

WIT: The face of freedom of speech, thank you very much.

JESTER: An ornament to represent and encourage everyone's desire to say whatever the hell they want!

GOOSEY: (*Shocked*) Language!

JESTER: (*Clarifying*) German.

GOOSEY: Huh?

RUBI: It's wonderful to meet all of you! I'm enchanted, really, but—

GOOSEY: (*Excited*) You are?! We are, too!

WINDY: Don't confuse the girl. (*To RUBI*) It's lovely to finally meet you, too. You are enchanting. And we are enchanted, we think.

RUBI: (*Laughing*) Yes. Well, I thought you might be. But what do you mean "you think?"

WINDY: We simply woke up one day with a desire to entertain the Master.

DIANA: Speak for yourself. I'm here to guard the Master.

KNIGHTLY: And I!

EVENTYR: (*Shaking her head*) Non quiblic et alve converitas. *(If you only knew...)*

GOOSEY: (*To RUBI*) You see, some of us woke knowing we were to entertain the Master, like Windy, Jester, Wit, and myself. Others, defend. Still others were to care for the castle or the Master properly, like Bergen, Leder, Dopple and Ganger (*THEY bow*).

RUBI: (*Indicating the state of the castle*) Then how did it get like this?

WINDY: The Castle used to be alive with more like us and then—

DIANA: Just after the Man died—

KNIGHTLY: No, it was before that.

DIANA: You think I don't remember when my Guard-mates returned to statues of bronze?

GOOSEY: Diana, I think Knightly means the day the Man brought you-know-what back with him (*indicating EVENTYR*).

EVENTYR: (*Sadly*) Mark forovisclimb, pear opratte mein golf. *(He was such a selfish man, if only he could have seen the cost!)*

WIT: Oh yeah, I remember! Stupid April the 12th of forever ago!

JESTER: That was the worst of all the days.

RUBI: What happened?

WIT: Weren't you listening? The Master's father brought that big *Goulish* painting into the Castle—

GOOSEY: (*Loyally*) She's Gaulish!

JESTER: —and one by one, the rest of everybody just went *Ppptth-bbttt* (*spitting*).

EVENTYR: (*Defensively*) Ar be gobben die fater et conlahbin gor fershmat. Frab giblie per persnisintat! (*With finality*) Don Din Dun. Resketin flor jibecag. (*I tried to tell him what would happen! I did, but he wouldn't hear of it. That was that. I wish I'd never met him!*)

GOOSEY: No one is saying it was your fault, Eventyr. The Man was being quite odd before that. Then suddenly, statues returned to being statues, the paintings, too. It was a matter of months before we stopped seeing him, too.

GNOMES: Now it's just us.

RUBI: I assumed there was some sort of spell, but mainly for food. (*EVENTYR snorts derisively*). You know...this sounds a lot like a story I heard as a child. Something about a monster and a fairy. (*Laughing*) Is there a trapped fairy somewhere in the castle?

EVENTYR: Forglobben klib (*whistles like "I'm right here!"*).

DIANA: Pretty sure we would have noticed a (*mocking voice*) *fairy*.

WIT: Nope. Just us and the big guy.

RUBI: You mean the beast?

> (*The CASTLE looks at each other, uncomfortable.*)

GOOSEY: We don't like to call him that.

RUBI: Oh. Does he have a name?

DIANA: He's the Master.

RUBI: He's not my master.

JESTER: Oh really? So who else do you work and slave for?

RUBI: He is my employer—though we were paid in advance. I'll not call anyone "Master".

GOOSEY: (*Keeping the peace*) We don't mean to upset you, Rubi.

WIT & JESTER: I do.

DIANA: Why does it matter what you call him? A little touchy for hired help, aren't you?

RUBI: (*Gaining steam.*) You know what? I may be hired help, but I'm still free. And even if this Beast thinks he is my master, he is not.

DIANA: Try telling him that.

WIT: Oo, oo, but do it where we can watch!

WINDY: (*To WIT*) Hush! (*To RUBI*) It's good to see a woman who knows her mind.

JESTER: If not her place.

RUBI: (*Turning on him*) Just because I stand in a place, that doesn't make it *my* place unless I choose to own it! (*Looks around*) If I owned this castle, you would be amazed at how things would change.

EVENTYR: (*Impressed*) While comber fell markzen. *(Now this is interesting.)*

DIANA: (*Unimpressed*) Pretty sure the Master owns this castle.

KNIGHTLY: (*Nervous*) He'd not be pleased one bit.

RUBI: As far as I can tell, the Beast doesn't care.

EVENTYR: (*Cautioning*) Vorlig von schlisel. Et garmin fortuna. *(Be careful, dear. We don't want trouble.)*

JESTER: (*Taunting*) So whatcha gonna do, little miss?

RUBI: I guess you'll see, Jester.

GOOSEY: Oh, please don't be angry with us, Rubi. Jester hasn't spoken to anyone with a heart in hundreds of years.

RUBI: I'm not angry. (*Smiles*) I'm sure we'll come to be great friends.

> (*JESTER, WIT, and DIANA scoff.*)

RUBI: (*To JESTER*) Friends who see me *own it* (*bows and exits*).

WIT: Whhaaatt just happened?

KNIGHTLY: I think you tossed the gauntlet, Wit.

DIANA: And now we'll get to see what this little girl is made of.

Vignette 6: Laundry Game

> (*Rubi is hanging laundry inside. CASTLE could be used to hold the clothes lines. BEAST enters from DSL and walks right into a sheet, becoming tangled because he wasn't looking where he was going.*)

BEAST: (*Confused*) What is all this?

RUBI: Clean laundry.

BEAST: (*Not able to see RUBI*) Take it down!

RUBI: It's snowing outside. It needs some place warm to dry.

BEAST: (*Growling*) I said take it down.

RUBI: Nope. (*Laughs, punching a sheet near him.*)

BEAST: (*Throws the sheet back; RUBI is not there*) Where are you?!

RUBI: (*Teasing*) I'm somewhere in this room...

BEAST: (*Yelling*) I don't like games!

RUBI: I don't like laundry. We all have our cross to bear. Playing won't kill you.

BEAST: I don't play. I stalk.

RUBI: Big talk, big guy.

> (*BEAST growls and takes off his cloak, hanging it on the banister. BEAST begins stalking her; hears a sound DSR.*)

RUBI: (*Jumps out from behind him*) Boo!

BEAST: (*Squeals*) AH!

> (*The CASTLE snickers; he glares. BEAST shushes the CASTLE and we see his animal side, catlike and prowley, but always just missing RUBI. She teases him, tricks him, and it does become a game. Finally they are "facing off," one on each side of a large sheet CENTER; a stalemate that turns into a dance. RUBI moves, and BEAST follows. RUBI pulls down the sheet and sticks her tongue out at BEAST, who, surprised, laughs. RUBI stops dancing, loving the sound. BEAST is embarrassed and rushes to EXIT.*)

Vignette 7: The Cloak

> (*The laundry is down. RUBI is dusting JESTER and WIT, humming and dancing.*)

WINDY: (*Wistfully, trying to mimic RUBI*) You are so graceful, Rubi.

RUBI: Thank you.

GOOSEY: Oh, I so appreciate your bright attitude!

JESTER: Almost as much as we appreciate the dusting and polishing.

WIT: I don't think my ears have been this clean in ages!

DIANA: Or ever.

KNIGHTLY: Wondrous indeed, the things we've been able to hear in the past month.

RUBI: Such as?

EVENTYR: (*Clearly*) The Master laughed.

> (*CASTLE gasps.*)

WINDY: (*Pointing at EVENTYR*) You spoke!

> (EVENTYR *nods, shocked and pleased.*)

WINDY: Real words! (*EVENTYR nods again, a little confused. WINDY rushes up the stairs, very close to EVENTYR*) Do it again.

> (EVENTYR *shrugs, shaking head "I don't know."*)

WINDY: Don't worry, darling. Just a little something.

EVENTYR: (*Trying it out*) The Master laughed like rocks tumbling on top of each other.

> (*WINDY moves down the stairs dramatically, winding up for a faint.*)

WINDY: Catch me Knightly! (*He does, assisting her to fall gracefully to the ground.*)

RUBI: Oh no, Windy! (*To KNIGHTLY*) What's the matter?

KNIGHTLY: Well, you've heard. Eventyr doesn't talk much. And when she does—

WIT: It's a mindless mishmash of marbled mumbling.

KNIGHTLY: Yes, thank you for reminding us, Wit.

GOOSEY: I wonder what changed.

DIANA: Ask her yourself, why don't you?

GOOSEY: I don't want to be nosey.

DIANA: Don't you? (*They share a significant look.*)

JESTER: (*Markedly changing the subject*) Rubi, there's been a hive of bees in the wall...so annoying!

KNIGHTLY: That's not bees, Jester. That's our Rubi humming.

WIT: Oh, that explains it.

JESTER: (*to RUBI*) Ugh! Stop it! It's so annoying!

WINDY: (*Suddenly comes to.*) I like it! Besides, how could she dance without music? (*To RUBI*) You've really been inspiring my poses since you've been here you know.

GOOSEY: Yes, making the Castle a lovely place to be again.

RUBI: (*Looking at the much improved room*) My mother did say I could see beauty wherever I am.

GOOSEY: I think you *make* beauty wherever you are.

EVENTYR: And I doubt we're the only ones that have noticed.

RUBI: Oh, I think you might be.

WINDY: Don't be so sure.

KNIGHTLY: You have brought softness into this castle, my lady. The Master hasn't been near as harsh as in days past. You did hear him laugh, didn't you?

RUBI: (*Smiling*) Do you really think that he—

BEAST: (*Roars from offstage*).

    (*RUBI drops her cloth; genuinely frightened.*)

BEAST: (*Enters USL, furious*) Where is my cloak?!

RUBI: (*Looks to the CASTLE, but they all shrug*) What cloak?

BEAST: *My* cloak! The one that I wear!

RUBI: You'll have to be more specific...

BEAST: (*Yelling*) Everything has always been where it always is until you came and now everything is moved and nothing is where it always was before!

RUBI: That didn't help...

BEAST: (*Roars*).

RUBI: (*Firmer*) Neither did that.

BEAST: (*Softer, but angry.*) It is a large green cloak. I wear it every single day. (*RUBI thinks, but he is impatient.*) It's this big (*motions with his arms*)!

RUBI: I'm sorry, I simply don't remember seeing it.

BEAST: Of course you don't. You're not really thinking, are you? Not about anything that matters.

RUBI: (*Taken aback*) That's not very nice.

BEAST: (*Pacing*) You make a maze of my Castle, putting things in ridiculous places. Changing things however you'd like. Selfish elbow biter. Did you do this at home? Is that why they sent you away?

RUBI: (*Near tears*) That's enough.

BEAST: (*Taunting*) Am I hurting your feelings? Maybe you should pick them up before someone steps on them.

RUBI: (*Loud and firm, but controlled.*) Don't talk to me like that.

    (*CASTLE gasps.*)

BEAST: (*Low and furious*) What did you say?

RUBI: I am working hard every single day. The fact that you cannot *see* the work I do is not my fault.

CASTLE: Hear, hear!

>   (*BEAST growls at them; RUBI blushes with gratitude.*)

RUBI: How can you not see how beautiful I have made it? (*Indicating the much-improved room.*)

BEAST: And I suppose beauty makes you special? Beauty is useless. You are useless.

RUBI: That's it. You will speak to me kindly or not at all.

BEAST: (*Standing to his full height*) How dare you—

RUBI: (*Standing to her full height*) How dare I what?

>   (*BEAST roars.*)

>   (*RUBI roars back.*)

>   (*BEAST is shocked into silence. RUBI holds up a finger, indicating "Please hold" and turns away from him.*)

>   (*RUBI roars again, out.*)

RUBI: Is this why you do it? (*She doesn't wait for him to answer.*

>   (*RUBI roars again, enjoying the power of her voice, turning it into her own "war cry," letting out all her pent up feelings. This should be very powerful. RUBI, in a rush of emotion and adrenaline feels a kinship with the BEAST, and turns to him.*)

RUBI: (*Laughing and understanding*) You must have a lot of feelings to yell like you do.

BEAST: (*Snarling*) I roar because I am a beast.

RUBI: (*Curious*) I think there is more to it...

BEAST: (*Angry*) You don't know!

RUBI: (*Pleading*) What don't I know?

BEAST: You've been pampered and praised, loved and protected! Your father cared enough to steal for you.

RUBI: (*Coldly*) You know nothing of my family.

BEAST: You win over even my castle. (*Furious.*) You've been doted on for your *beauty*. (*Like it's a bad word*) Beauty is over-rated.

RUBI: (*She straightens up, standing with strength, shouting with glorious confidence.*) I am not ashamed to be beautiful!

BEAST: You should be.

RUBI: (*Laughing at him*) Who says?

BEAST: My mother!

RUBI: (*Taken aback*) Oh. (*Uncomfortable, but not willing to lose ground.*) Well, I don't know what she told you, but I do know that *seeing* beauty makes me grateful and happy and...human. It makes me *want* to live! Does anger do that for you?

(*BEAST growls.*)

RUBI: (*Quieter, but just as strong*) Despite what others may think, I am not nothing. (*BEAST bows his head, embarrassed.*) I deserve to be treated well. So you...be nice.

BEAST: You don't understand anything (*Exits through the main doors.*)

RUBI: (*Yelling after him*) JUST BE NICE! Arg! (*Roars and stomps around for a minute. Then sits, thinking.*)

GOOSEY: (*In awe*) I can't believe you spoke to him like that.

DIANA: Good on you.

RUBI: (*Frustrated*) He's just so...he reminds me of my father. And my brother and my sisters!

WIT: Were they hairy and mean, too?

RUBI: No. But it was this idea they had that I could be stepped on and it wouldn't hurt me. When I was little, there was a morning room where I would go to play alone. But Gelde, Perle, and Thors called me a selfish baby and complained to my mother. Mama said it would calm discord in the house if I just changed to please the others. I never found the morning room empty after that.

KNIGHTLY: Forgive me, but I don't see the similarity.

RUBI: Don't you? I'll simplify. Rubi makes a pretty place for her to be herself. Then, a *store tyran (big tyrant)* mocks her and she must change for them.

JESTER: There! Now I see it.

WINDY: You wanted harmony in your family.

RUBI: Yes!

EVENTYR: But how can there be harmony when only one instrument is playing?!

RUBI: I'm not doing it this time. I've made something pleasant here, something magical! He's not a Master of anything. He's just a spoiled bully.

WINDY: Careful, Rubi.

RUBI: I don't care if he hears me!

GOOSEY: We do.

RUBI: (*Disbelief*) Why?

WINDY: (*Pause, deciding how much to tell her.*) He has been hurt.

RUBI: Is that supposed to excuse it?

EVENTYR: Of course not. He could choose differently. Yet...

RUBI: What?

EVENTYR: A rose bush has thorns because it learned it needed to protect its blossoms. (*RUBI looks confused*) So it is with many people. Hurt people ... well, they hurt people.

RUBI: (Looking after the BEAST) I can see that. (Determined) So he hurts. It doesn't give him permission to treat me that way. If me being wonderful and happy bothers him that much, he can send me away. I'm not going to change for him.

EVENTYR: You already have, actually.

DIANA: I'll say.

EVENTYR: You came here a quiet, forgettable girl.

WIT: A jellyfish!

EVENTYR: But now you roar and speak your mind all without fear. What was it you said earlier?

JESTER: "Owning it?"

RUBI: (*Laughs.*) I suppose that's true. It doesn't make sense. I mean, I'm basically a prisoner. So why do I feel so free?

EVENTYR: (S*miling*) That sounds rhetorical.

RUBI: (*Amazed*) I have changed.

EVENTYR: Now give him the space to change, too.

RUBI: Maybe I can help him.

DIANA: (*scoffs*)

KNIGHTLY: Just lead the way, Rubi.

GOOSEY: And be kind.

EVENTYR: I suspect even a little kindness would go a long way.

> (*Lights change/dim. RUBI searches for the CLOAK and finds it tossed on the banister, just behind where the*

BEAST had been standing. She laughs and looks at the door, thinking.)

(Lights up. RUBI has set a small meal with two plates near the BEAST's chair by the fire. RUBI watches as the BEAST enters from the main doors. He's a mess. He walks around the room, taking note of the fine pillows on the repaired chaise, the clean floor, the flowers on the mantle and the lack of dust on the banisters. He ends near the fire, seeing the food laid out for him. Humbled and embarrassed, he curls up into his chair like a hurt dog. RUBI comes down the stairs, carrying the cloak. BEAST hears her but doesn't turn around.)

BEAST: (*Softly*) I didn't think you would still be here.

RUBI: (*Nervous; playfully*) Surprise. (*BEAST doesn't answer.*) I found your cloak.

BEAST: Where was it?

RUBI: On the banister, just there.

BEAST: (*Chuckles*) Of course it was. (*RUBI sets the cloak beside him; he doesn't look at her and she moves to EXIT*) I'm sorry.

RUBI: (*Stops and smiles*) Thank you.

> *(BEAST looks at her, she looks at him. He looks away, cleaning out his coat.)*

RUBI: May I help you?

BEAST: No. I don't need help.

RUBI: (*Puzzled by the pain in his voice, pauses*) You can't reach your back, you know. There is a great big branch right...here...

BEAST: Don't touch me!

RUBI: I'm sorry.

BEAST: I don't need your pity.

RUBI: (*Gently*) It's not pity. I'm here to take care of the castle and...those inside it.

BEAST: No one *wants* to help a beast!

RUBI: I don't mind helping you.

BEAST: I'm not worth helping.

RUBI: Everyone is worth helping.

BEAST: You are here to care for the castle. Not me.

RUBI: (*Pauses at his sadness; then shrugs*) You can't stop me. It's no use.

BEAST: What?

RUBI: I want to help you because...you are a rose (*looks up to EVEN-TYR*) uh, I mean...(*she moves closer to him*) I see beauty wherever I am.

BEAST: (*Hopeful*) Do you? (*Reaches out to touch her*) Will you marry me? *(RUBI recoils at his hand. BEAST turns away, sad and embarrassed.)* You are free to go.

RUBI: But—

BEAST: I release you. I'll consider the debt repaid if you just leave now.

RUBI: But I...

BEAST: Go.

> (*Frantic to have another chance, RUBI gets an idea. She picks up a plate from the table and drops it, breaking it.*)

BEAST: (*Shocked*) What did you do that for?

RUBI: I'm still in debt.

BEAST: Get out of here.

> (*RUBI breaks another*).

BEAST: (*Confused*) What are you doing?!

RUBI: (*Smiling playfully, hopefully*) I have to stay. I'm still in debt.

BEAST: (*Concerned she will break more dishes*) I suppose you must? (*RUBI smiles, relieved*) I don't understand you.

RUBI: And I don't understand you. So we're even. (*BEAST hangs his head.*) Look, you don't have to send me away just because I won't marry you. We could be...friends?

BEAST: (*Firmly*) I am a monster, Rubi. I always have been. You can't change me.

RUBI: (*Agreeing*) No one changes unless they want it for themselves.

BEAST: (*Grunts*) Help me get this stuff out of my quills. (*He sits, his back to her. RUBI waits.*) Please?

RUBI: Of course. Hold still.

(*Lights out on her helping him by the fire.*)

END OF ACT I

47

ACT II

Scene 1: Kleiner Weiler, Germany

(Lights up on a German Hamlet early in the morning. Vosen's Bakery is putting out bread and GLENA is pushing the sweet smell out the door. SAFFI is setting tables outside the Wunder Bar, with small vases of blue flowers. Her son, EMIL sets cups on the table with a small tablecloth. FRITZ is playing music while a few townspeople dance to the tune. HEDDA and ALBERTE are setting out a table of goods they sell from their mercantile, deeply discounted. CLARA and ANKA hang dresses, trousers and pinafores on their lattice stand up shop downstage of the mercantile, and set up stools to sew — showing themselves as seamstresses. RASMUS enters from USR and crosses to the fountain, looking puzzled at the letter in his possession. As HE thinks, he smells the bread and goes to buy. RUBI enters DSL by CLARA and ANKA in a cloak, carrying a bag that she will use to take home the plates she has come to purchase.)

RUBI: *(Inhales deeply)* What is that delightful smell?

ANKA: Well, it certainly isn't me.

CLARA: It's either the bakery or the Wunder Bar (*Voonder Bar*).

RUBI: I've never smelled anything like it!

ANKA: *(Looking her over)* You aren't from around here are you?

RUBI: No. Well, I am from around here now.

CLARA: *(Laughing)* I see.

ANKA: I don't.

48

RUBI: (*Clarifying*) I have lived near here for nearly six months, but this is my first trip to...what is this town called?

ANKA/CLARA: Kleiner Weiler (Klie-na Vie-la).

RUBI: Klia-na Vie-ler?

ANKA: Perfect. We can barely tell you are Danish.

RUBI: Is my accent that bad?

CLARA: No, it's your use of red.

RUBI: (*Laughing*) Ah, we *are* partial to reds.

ANKA: (*Motioning to their clothes*) we are partial to blue and green here.

RUBI: And my name *is* Rubi.

CLARA: That is precious! I am Clara and this is my cousin, Anka. We are seamstresses.

RUBI: Pleased to meet you both.

CLARA: What brings you to town? I'm surprised you haven't needed to come before for supplies.

ANKA: Or clothes...

GLENA: (*Calling across the town*) Or bread! (*Everyone laughs.*)

ANKA: (*Territorial*) She's talking to us, Glena!

GLENA: Only because my breads drew her into town! (*Walks over to RUBI*) I am Glena Vosen. I'm the one who bakes the bread.

ANKA: (*Grumpy*) And frosts my cookies.

GLENA: (*Putting an arm around her*) Oh, don't be like that Anka! We have a symbiotic relationship. I bake bread and delicious things, the people in town get fatter...they buy more clothes from you.

ANKA: Huh...I hadn't thought of it like that.

CLARA: But how do we help you, Glena?

GLENA: You make clothes so people don't have to buy their strudel naked! (*Some laugh, some are shocked.*)

SAFFI: You are quite shocking, Glena.

GLENA: You love me anyway. (*To RUBI*) Now, our *schöne fremde*, what brings you to town today?

RUBI: Neither bread nor fine dresses, I'm afraid. I have come to purchase plates. I broke a number of ours...um, the Master's. (*Not wanting to reveal too much*) Uh, I have broken some plates.

GLENA: (*Caught the slip*) Ah...well then you'll want to come to the Mercantile. Run by the stout and friendly Kramer Sisters, Hedda and Alberte.

HEDDA: Did you just refer to me as STOUT?

GLENA: *And* friendly!

EMIL: (*Sniffing from SR*) Is something burning?

GLENA: My *Franzbrötchen*! (*FRANS bro shen*) (*GLENA leaves RUBI behind to save her cinnamon cakes. Everyone laughs. She pokes her head back out the door to save face.*) They aren't burned, they are matured!

FRITZ: No, they're burnt!

HEDDA: (*Laughing at GLENA*) How can we help you this morning Frauline—?

RUBI: Rubi Smuk. I am in need of some plates. We—er—I have broken a few and need replacements. Do you have any that might match this pattern? (*Pulls a plate from her satchel. HEDDA looks it over and hands it to her sister, ALBERTE.*)

ALBERTE: (*Excited*) Oh my! What is this? I've never seen something like it up close. Are these hand painted cornflowers?!

50

HEDDA: (*Awed*) They are, Alberte! Dear me! (*Back to RUBI*) Where did you come by such fine tableware?

RUBI: I'm not sure.

ALBERTE: I'm sure I'd remember.

RUBI: (*Honestly*) I wish I did know the history. Are they quite fine? (*THEY both nod enthusiastically.*) Do you have anything to match? (*They shake their heads dismally.*) Oh.

ALBERTE: We used to carry such things.

RUBI: Oh! (*Hopefully*) Will you again?

HEDDA: No one can say for sure. (*Covertly*) There has been a band of hooligans on the roads for the past three months.

ALBERTE: More like six! They have been stealing our orders before they ever get here. We haven't had a proper shipment in half a year!

RUBI: That's terrible! I'm so sorry.

HEDDA: If they'd intercepted one or two, that would be terrible. It has been going on for months. It's simply the end of everything. And not just our things! Kleiner Weiler used to be a prosperous town, and growing. We're on the way to the Harz Mountains you know, to Berlin and Bavaria!

RASMUS: Now no one will travel the dangerous road to our village. We can barely provide for ourselves.

SAFFI: Stop painting such a dismal picture, Rasmus Verloren!

SMITH: Those are the colors we have, Saffi. I don't even know how you keep the Wunderbar. I haven't had to put hammer to anvil in over a month.

SAFFI: There are plenty of fowl in the forest. My son Emil is a good shot for a mallard or two, aren't you dear?

EMIL: (*Shy, he simply nods*).

SAFFI: That reminds me, we have need of a new oven handle, Smith. We can trade. Our garden has a good yield, if you'd like some veg.

SMITH: I'd rather a good stew.

SAFFI: With the bandits on the road, it will be slim; but I bet I can get up a tasty something with what I've got.

GLENA: (*Re-entering from the bakery*) All is well! The *Franzbrötchen* are safe, soft, cinnamon-y and for sale! (*No one moves.*) What are we talking about?

ALBERTE: The hooligans.

GLENA: Those ruffians are lucky I've not gotten my hands on them.

SAFFI: Don't stir up trouble with them, Glena. I'm sure we'll be fine until the soldiers come.

GLENA: (*Scoffs*) We've sent four letters so far and not heard a peep. Without a signet seal, we're just not being noticed.

HEDDA: There was that one man in town two months back—

GLENA: Offering "insurance" if we pay in? As if we weren't poor enough! It's highway robbery! Well, you know what I mean.

RUBI: (*Concerned*) Do you all suffer from the thieves?

SAFFI: (*Comfortingly*) Business has dropped off substantially, frauline. But don't you mind that. We have enough to feed...

ANKA: And clothe...

HEDDA: And stock...

GLENA: And fatten!

SAFFI: A few passersby. Like you!

RUBI: You are all very kind. I wish I could partake of everything you have. But I only have enough to pay for plates. (*They hide their disappointment.*)

HEDDA: I will see what we have in our storage room to match your plates. It may not be quite as fine, but perhaps we will be lucky!

RUBI: Thank you. (*The town goes back to normal; rather sleepy. She sees Rasmus, who is sitting on the fountain, looking puzzled.*) Are you all right?

RASMUS: Oh, better than most of the *menschen*. The post is one thing the brigands don't mess with, because it would surely bring soldiers.

RUBI: Then what are you doing with your face?

RASMUS: I am conveying expressions and enhancing the messages of my words. (*Pulling faces as he talks*).

RUBI: (*Laughing; RASMUS laughs, too.*) I meant, why do you look puzzled?

RASMUS: It is good to say what you mean, isn't it?

RUBI: Indeed.

RASMUS: (*Pulling out a letter*) I'm the postman here, you see. I know everyone and everywhere in town. I've been here since it was built! But this one confounds me.

RUBI: I'll be no help. This is my first time here.

RASMUS: So I heard. Where are you from?

RUBI: *Aarhus*, Denmark originally.

RASMUS: *Aarhus*, you say?

RUBI: Yes.

RASMUS: That is where this letter is from!

RUBI: Oh...may I see it? (*RASMUS shrugs and hands it over. RUBI pales*) This is for me.

RASMUS: You are Rubi Smuk?

RUBI: Yes. Where did this come from?

RASMUS: It was left at the Wunderbar four months ago by a passing family. It has become quite the puzzle for me. Look at that address! Didn't they know where you were?

RUBI: They must have been scared off searching for me. The bandits.

RASMUS: Ah.

HEDDA: (*Shouts happily*) We found something, Frauline! Feast your eyes on these, Rubi, and see if they won't compliment the cornflowers quite nicely.

ALBERTE: Not a perfect match but...

RUBI: Oh, they are lovely! What is the cost.

HEDDA: They are also bone china, and there are six.

RUBI: That is splendid! In case I break more. The price?

ALBERTE: Seventeen guldens.

RUBI: I have twenty.

HEDDA: Anything else for you, frauline? A brooch perhaps.

RUBI: Oh, I could not. I can only spend money on the plates.

HEDDA: A gift then. For an honest woman.

RUBI: *Mange tak.*

HEDDA: (*Correcting her*) *Danke shön*. You are in Germany now.

ALBERTE: And your change.

RUBI: *Danke shön.*

GLENA: *(Carrying a fresh roll and a basket)* I don't know where you are going, but take a *Franzbrötchen* with you, for the road.

SAFFI: *(Handing her a gourd)* And some water.

RUBI: Oh, I couldn't!

GLENA: We may be getting poorer in a few things, but kindness we have in spades.

ANKA: Hear, hear!

RUBI: *(Touched)* I'm so glad I came to town today. And that we met. *Danke shön*, my new friends. I'm sure I'll see you again. May your fortunes improve!

CLARA: Be careful on your way!

RASMUS: I hope it is only good news.

RUBI: Danke. I hope so, too.

(Exit. Lights out.)

SCENE 2: THE CASTLE

(Curtain lifts and lights up on the interior of the castle, which looks far better than at the end of the first act. BEAST is trying to fix the door he slammed at the end of the first act, which was hanging off the hinge. DI-ANA and KNIGHTLY are under him, making sure he doesn't fall and hurt himself. The GNOMES are handing him tools.)

DIANA: Master, should you really be doing that? You have no head for this kind of thing. It is Rubi's duty now at any rate.

KNIGHTLY: That's rather an uncivilized view, Diana.

DIANA: Because she's a girl or because you're living in the medieval era?

BEAST: *(Straining)* I just...want to...make it nice...for her. Like you said.

DIANA: I never said anything of the sort.

GOOSEY: He means me.

DIANA: Oh. What did you tell him?

BEAST: That being nice to someone is nicer than not being nice.

WIT: Eh?

GOOSEY: What I actually suggested was that the Master make Rubi a meal some night because, as a grand philosopher once said "The Sauce of Service is Sweeter than the Sprinkling Salt-Shaker of Self-Servitude."

WIT: You made that up.

GOOSEY: *(Convinced she's right)* No I didn't. It's a thing.

JESTER: A thing you made up.

56

WINDY: I think it's admirable that the Master is making an effort for Rubi.

DIANA: Why should he, though?

BEAST: (*Frustrated that he can't get the door to set*) I want her to stay, curse the blazes! I want her to be happy, and like it here, and like me, and want to stay. (*The door sets and he falls over with excitement!*) Aha!! You see—she'll like that! Won't she? (*CASTLE shrugs.*) Surely *this* will show her how I feel.

> (*RUBI enters, carrying the plates and bread and drink the town sent back with her. The GNOMES help with the things, as BEAST tries to show off the fixed door. He is disheartened by her lack of notice.*)

BEAST: Did you find the village well enough? (*RUBI doesn't answer.*) Was the walk too tiring? I'm sure opening this door was easy as breathing! Eh?

RUBI: What? Oh, I'm sorry. I need a moment alone. (*Exits with the letter.*)

BEAST: (*Watches her; upset.*) What else can I do?

KNIGHTLY: Be kind?

> (BEAST *growls.*)

DIANA: (*Reconciled to his desire, decides to offer advice*) Give her a sword.

BEAST: A what?

DIANA: Every good woman should have her own sword.

WINDY: A new dress.

DIANA: (*Firmly*) A sword.

KNIGHTLY: Come now, what would Rubi really care for?

57

JESTER: The Master to wear a bag on his head?

WINDY: What makes you think she's not happy here, Master?

BEAST: Well, for one thing, THAT! (*Motioning after RUBI.*)

GOOSEY: She did break the plates didn't she?

BEAST: Yes.

GOOSEY: That shows she wants to stay.

BEAST: It just shows she didn't want to leave.

EVENTYR: I think it's possible she even likes you.

BEAST: (*X-ing to sit in his chair buy the fireplace*.) Don't. Don't do that.

EVENTYR: I only meant—

BEAST: It doesn't matter what she thinks about me. I can't worry about that. What matters is that I like her. I think she will stay if she is happy. I have to make her happy somehow...

EVENTYR: I'm not convinced she is UNhappy.

BEAST: You saw her when she came back. I knew I should not have let her go to the village. She found the people there better company than me.

WIT: Can you blame her?

BEAST: (*Roaring, he crosses the stage*) I'm trying, aren't I? (*Picks up a pillow from the chaise and is about to throw it when he just flops down like a child.*)

GOOSEY: (*Calming*) Of course you are. We've all seen it, haven't we?

KNIGHTLY: Though, perhaps—

BEAST: (*Rounding on him, crouched on the back of the chaise*) What?

KNIGHTLY: (*Wisely*) A lady responds to a gallant gentleman taking an interest in her interests.

WINDY: How would you know?

DIANA: He probably read it somewhere. (*KNIGHTLY glares at her.*)

BEAST: (*Resigned, sitting like a gentleman.*) What would you suggest?

GOOSEY: Well, she likes people.

KNIGHTLY: She likes to dance.

BERGEN: And cook...

WINDY: You know what that means!

BEAST: No.

WINDY: A party!

BEAST: No way!

WINDY: A party would be perfect!

LEDER: (*Clarifying*) We meant that you could cook with her.

KNIGHTLY: Or dance with her.

WINDY: Well, *I* meant a party.

BEAST: (*Pacing*) Not in a dozen centuries would I ever consider it, not for anyone; I don't care how they make me feel or—(*RUBI walks in*) whether it's raining in Bavaria.

WIT: That didn't make any sense.

DIANA: Sometimes I wish you had a full head so I could smack you upside it.

JESTER: No, *that* didn't make any sense.

BEAST: Shush!

RUBI: (*Enters, tying a work apron on, ready to fix the door*) The plates weren't an exact match, but I did the best I could.

WINDY: I'm sure you did, dear.

RUBI: (*Finally seeing the BEAST*) What are you doing down here?

BEAST: (*Fumbling*) I was...the door.

RUBI: (*Tries the door, pleased it works.*) Oh that's marvelous! But that was my duty, sir.

BEAST: I wanted to help. You are offended?

RUBI: Not in the least.

BEAST: But you are upset. (*RUBI looks down.*) Is it because you had to come back?

RUBI: (*Surprised*) No! I just, I had a few things on my mind.

WINDY: Such as?

RUBI: This village—you would have loved it, Windy! So charming, and warm, full of kind, odd people. But the village is in some trouble.

GOOSEY: How?

RUBI: There are hooligans on the roads into and out of the village, stealing their goods, scaring off the tourists. They can't make a living like that.

KNIGHTLY: Haven't they some sort of militia to handle the ruffians?

RUBI: Glena—the baker—told me that they have to hire soldiers from the Kaiser, but with the money short, they can't. Worst of all, they are so kind.

WINDY: How can that be the worst part?

RUBI: They have so little. Yet they gave me food and drink to walk home, and advice and I just...I wish I could help them somehow.

BEAST: (*sniffing the basket she brought back*) Ah.

RUBI: And...(*pauses*) I received a letter from my family. (*She crosses to the chaise DR and sits, pulling out the letter.*)

WINDY: Bad news?

RUBI: Not exactly. My father, well, you know the kind of man my father was. He has upset enough of the wrong people, so my family took the opportunity to move. To Belgium. Without me. (*She pauses, looking at the letter.*) Just like they always dreamed. (*Pauses.*) They left this on their way. (*Disbelief*) They didn't even stop to see me.

BEAST: You wish you could be with them.

RUBI: (*Slowly, feeling herself out; honestly*) No. I don't. And if they didn't care to see me, then it must be all right that I don't mind not seeing them. (*She laughs, then covers her face with her hand, overcome with emotion. BEAST looks to CASTLE and they motion for him to do a variety of things. To touch her, to sit next to her, to kneel by her, etc. BEAST tries to follow their silent direction at one point perching on the back of the chaise behind her and the CASTLE wordlessly try to get him down. BEAST, confused, settles for:*)

BEAST: There, there.

RUBI: Danke. I'm alright.

BEAST: No, you're not.

RUBI: I suppose not quite.

JESTER & WIT: That rhymed!

CASTLE: Shhhh!

BEAST: What would make you feel better?

RUBI: Time, most likely. Keeping busy.

BEAST: (*Relieved.*) Oh good. So not a party then.

RUBI: (*Laughing*) A party? (*Thoughtful*) A party. (*Excited*) A party!

BEAST: No, *not* a party.

RUBI: That might be just the thing!

BEAST: You said *not* a party. *Not a party* is just the thing.

RUBI: Don't you see? We could help everyone!

BEAST: How could a party help anyone? I'd rather just give them money and send them on their way.

RUBI: Well, you could do that, too!

BEAST: Hmph.

RUBI: Preparing a party would busy me, lift their spirits, *and* repay them for their kindness.

BEAST: Wait! You mean have a party *here?*

RUBI: (*Slowing down*) Yes.

BEAST: You don't see a problem with that?

RUBI: (*Stands, optimistic*) Not at all! (*RUBI goes about the room envisioning updates and changes and decorations.*) We could have this spiffed up in no time! I've finished most of the major repairs. We could bring back the banquet table and chairs, with some benches for conversation set round the room. I'm sure they have musicians— they could set up on the landing there and play—filling the room with music! There will be dancing and merriment and the chandelier aglow with candles.

    (*CASTLE is staring at RUBI.*)

RUBI: What?

JESTER: Don't you see a big,

WIT: Hairy,

62

JESTER: *Beastly* problem with having the party here? (*BEAST looks embarrassed, but doesn't correct JESTER.*)

RUBI: (*Walks back down the stairs.*) No. I don't see a problem. (*Looking right at him.*)

BEAST: Well I do. And they will.

WIT: Like I said, Master. Paper bag over the head works wonders!

RUBI: That's it!

GOOSEY: Rubi! Don't hurt the Master's feelings.

RUBI: That's not what I meant. A masquerade!

DIANA: A what?

RUBI: It's a party where everyone wears a costume and masks, the more lavish the better. I once attended a Masquerade in Copenhagen as a horse!

KNIGHTLY: Splendid!

JESTER: I'm sure it suited you.

DIANA: Pipe down, pine brain.

WINDY: Oh what a marvelous idea! (*CASTLE agrees.*)

BEAST: No one would know that I'm—?

RUBI: No one would know. They would think you are just like them.

EVENTYR: And in a way, you are.

BEAST: Bah. I wouldn't know what to do.

RUBI: All anyone will do is eat and dance.

BEAST: I can do half of those things.

RUBI: (*Innocently*) Which half? (*BEAST gives her a look.*) Don't worry. I can teach you. The Danish dance is much like the German one; Come, I'll show you.

BEAST: There's no music.

> (*EVENTYR begins playing music. CASTLE turns to stare. BEAST glares at her. EVENTYR just smiles.*)

RUBI: Come now. It's simple. Knightly and Diana can join us.

DIANA: I don't dance.

WINDY: Oh, let me!

RUBI: Well, watch first. See here, first we just walk in a circle, one two three, one two three, one two three, out and in. Turn and go the other way. One two three, one two three, one two three, out and in. (*Dancing over to him*) Then we waltz.

BEAST: You mean *walk*.

RUBI: (*Pronouncing more slowly*) *Waltz*. In counts of three, watch my feet. One, two, three, One, two, three, One, two, three. See? (*BEAST repeats the movement.*) First, in place. One, two, three, One, two, three. Then we move forward: One, two, three, One, two, three. And then we waltz together. (*RUBI raises her arms for the BEAST to hold her, and he is at a loss*).

BEAST: Together?

RUBI: Yes. You put your hand on my waist.

BEAST: You mean my paw.

RUBI: (*Gently*) I said what I meant.

BEAST: (*Confused*) Aren't you afraid?

RUBI: Do I look frightened of you? (*BEAST goes towards her, putting a hand on her waist, his downstage hand limp at his side. RUBI*

reaches out and takes it, lifting their hands to where they should be.)
Yes. Just like this. Now. One, two, three, One, two, three, One, two,
three (*They fall into a rhythm and begin spinning. Some leeway can
be taken with the dance here as they find their groove. They end DL,
very connected.*)

RUBI: (*A little dazed*) It's really wonderful with more people.

BEAST: I can't imagine how it could be.

RUBI: (*Smiles shyly*) Well, the colors and the dresses. And I've only
taught you half the dance...

BEAST: (*Pulls away from her and bows, kissing her hand.*) I look forward to our next lesson.

RUBI: So you mean...?

BEAST: We shall have a party. Invite the entire countryside if you'd
like. As long as you will dance with me.

RUBI: It will be my great pleasure, sir. (*Curtsey and laugh.*)

(*Lights out.*)

SCENE 3: KLEINER WEILER

(Lights up. GUNTER is standing on the fountain, Center, making an announcement to the town, CLARA, GLENA, SAFFI, SMITH, and ANKA are paying attention; others are giving half an ear.)

GUNTER: My name is Franz Aben, as I said folks, and for just a single gulden coin a week, I can insure the safety of your goods to town!

CLARA: (*To ANKA*) It sounds too good to be true!

GLENA: (*to SAFFI*) Then it probably is.

GUNTER: For just one gulden coin a week, Frauline (*to HEDDA*) I can see dishes and soaps, candles and flint delivered on time! (*to SMITH*) And you, mein herr! For the simple payment of a gulden a week, I will clear the bridges outside town and you will have more ferrier work than you could ever dream!

SMITH: I haven't shoed a horse in over a month. My bellows have nearly forgot how to keep a fire goin'.

ANKA: (*to SMITH, sweetly*) Mine could use a new set, Smith.

CLARA: He won't ask you to the Wunder Bar just because you shoe your pony every five weeks, Anka.

ANKA: He might.

GUNTER: I can tell you are all good, hard working mensch and what the bandits are doing to you all is a travesty! Frau Vosen (*to GLENA*), I've tasted your pies and rolls! They are the best this side of the Harz Mountains!

GLENA: *Sie konnen, das veeder sagen*! (You can say that again).

GUNTER: The Germanic kingdoms need such delectable scrumptu-ousness-es-es.

RASMUS: Too many S's.

GUNTER: I can protect not only your goods for travel, but the roads themselves! Think of it! More tourists than you can shake a stick at!

SMITH: How will you protect our village? You are just one man!

GUNTER: I have been hired by many nearby villages over the years to negotiate with hooligans in a language they understand.

GLENA: Negotiate? That doesn't sound like a solution.

SAFFI: It would be more peaceful than fighting.

GUNTER: There are other ways, you know. I lay traps. Trick them.

SMITH: What kind of traps?

GUNTER: You pay in, my friend, and you will find out.

CLARA: Money is tight, Herr Aben. Could we not pay you after the tourists return to our town?

GUNTER: You could wait until the cows return to town, Frau, but for my services, you must pay. A simple gulden, my friends. Is that too much to restore Kleiner Weiler to its prosperous state?

RASMUS: We should just wait until the soldiers come.

GUNTER: Ah, but my friends, it costs so much to keep a regiment here! Or you could simply pay one gulden to me, and all your problems would be solved.

> (ANKA, CLARA, HEDDA, and SAFFI move forward grudgingly to give GUNTER their money but are interrupted as RUBI and the BEAST enter town. RUBI is wearing a mask and a fine gown. The TOWN makes way for their entrance, curious and impressed.)

RUBI: People of Kleiner Weiler, gather 'round!

GLENA: (*Sarcastically*) Oh good, the gypsies have come to town. Go back to Romania!

RUBI: (*Laughing*) I'm not from Romania, *meine Frau*!

ANKA: I know that accent...

RUBI: We have come from the castle in the wood, to invite one and all to a Masquerade Ball!

    (*Excitement.*)

SAFFI: Who is doing this inviting?

ANKA: (*On the tip of her tongue*) I tell you, I know who that is, it's—

(*RUBI removes her mask*)

CLARA: Rubi Smuk!

ANKA: I knew it was her!

SAFFI: Rubi! You've returned!

    (*ALL run to embrace her.*)

CLARA: So glad you made it where you were headed safely.

GLENA: We worried about you, you know.

SAFFI: And now you've returned!

CLARA: That is a sensational gown! Where did you get it?!

RUBI: Do you like it? It was a gift from my friend, ... (*motioning to BEAST, suddenly realizing she doesn't know his name. BEAST slowly moves forward to stand near RUBI*).

ANKA: (*screaming in horror*) Oh my! (*BEAST cowers back*) Who dressed you?! (*ALL laugh*)

BEAST: (*Sincerely*) I did. Stevard Sholtze. I am from Gefangen Castle east of here.

RASMUS: Gefangen is not a castle! It's a pile of rubble.

EMIL: It's haunted!

SAFFI: It's not haunted, sweetheart.

EMIL: Is too! Monsters live at Gefangen. Papa told me so! (*BEAST shrinks, RUBI puts a hand on his arm. BANDITS begin to enter from SR behind the VILLAGERS.*)

SAFFI: Emil, Your Papa thought he invented water.

RUBI: I have been living at Gefangen for nearly a year, and I promise you, it is not haunted nor is it in ruins any longer. We (*motioning to BEAST*) have been repairing it.

BEAST: Rubi has done most of the work, actually.

RUBI: You have been helping me (*BEAST begins to argue*) No, you have. Take credit.

BEAST: (*Bashful*) We have brought the castle back to a semblance of its former glory.

GLENA: (*Scoffing*) That I'd like to see.

BEAST: You are invited to see—all of you!

RUBI: We invite you to a Masquerade Ball on Saturday next. A fantastic party hosted at Gefangen Castle by Lord Stevard Sholtze.

GUNTER: (*Breaking into the group*) It is dangerous! The roads are not safe. They are treacherous. (*Pointedly to his men*) Impassable.

(TOWN *chatters*.)

BEAST: No, I assure you! The ways to Gefangen are clear and safe.

GUNTER: The only safe roads are the roads I make safe.

RUBI: (*Suspiciously*) Don't I know you from somewhere?

BEAST: (*Powerfully, to GUNTER*) You have my word: the path to my castle is safe for all.

> (*GUNTER scrambles away. SMITH shakes BEAST's paw, examining his massive hand and leads him to the Wunderbar. ANKA follows, admiring his cloak. The BANDITS move UL as RUBI and VILLAGERS move DCL.*)

RUBI: Hedda, are you all paying into this man's scheme?

HEDDA: We cannot afford to...

ALBERTE: But we really can't afford *not* to, either, sister.

RUBI: Is it a gulden for the town per week?

CLARA: No, it is a gulden a week from each of us. Whoever pays will be protected, he says.

RUBI: And you know this man? Can you trust him?

GLENA: I don't trust him any farther than I can throw him. (*Watching GUNTER talk with his men*) Actually, not farther than Anka could throw him.

ANKA: (*Turning*) I heard that.

GLENA: (*Snappish*) Of course you did; you have ears like the eyes of a hawk! (*ANKA gives a high squeal of protest*) And the squeal of a piglet.

ANKA: (*Angry*) Why you ...

GLENA: Don't pick a fight you can't finish, precious.

CLARA: (*Coming between them, soothingly*) Stop egging her on, Glena. (*To ANKA*) Leave it alone; she's only joking.

GLENA: I'm sorry, Anka and Clara.

HEDDA: (*To RUBI*) You see how the strain wears on us all? Perhaps one gulden a week isn't really so much.

RUBI: But for how long, my friends? All of you paying for a month, well; there are what, seven shops in town?

GLENA: Nine, if you count the post.

RUBI: How much does it cost to bring soldiers to Kliener Wieler, Rasmus?

RASMUS: (*Thinking*) To station a battalion here, I believe, would cost over thirty Guldens every three months!

RUBI: (*Satisfied*) You'd pay 36 to that man in a single month for his protection.

SMITH: (*Impressed*) We should have thought of that.

GLENA: You'd think with all the baking I do, I'd have been able to come up with the math myself. (*To RASMUS*) Rasmus, you never told us what it would cost to settle a regiment here!

RASMUS: (*Defensive*) Nobody asked! (*Serious*) The real problem is getting attention on the request. Only a landlord's seal makes it past all the gatekeepers to someone who matters.

RUBI: A lord, you say?

RASMUS: Yes.

ANKA: (*Sarcastically*) Anyone know a hoity-toity upper-crustman who'd be willing to put his mark to a such a letter? I sure don't.

> (*The TOWN is crestfallen. RUBI, however has an idea. She crosses to BEAST, pulling him DR. GUNTER and his men are DL, talking in a loose huddle, careful not to be heard by the town.*)

FREIDA: I've *been* putting the pressure on, boss. Haven't we all?

LARS: Every road is watched, Gunter.

GUNTER: Don't call me that! I think that girl may know me.

FREIDA: Which one?

GUNTER: The fancy one.

FREIDA: She looks familiar.

GUNTER: Then be extra careful to not say my name, if you please.

HELMUT: Ja mein herr.

GUNTER: (*Accusingly*) They say there is a grand castle nearby. Why wasn't I told?

FREIDA: Nothing fine or dandy for miles around, *Franz* (*says the fake name markedly*). Just the same old village huts you'd find in any town.

LARS: (*Adding*) Except the haunted one.

HANSEL: Yes, except the haunted one.

GUNTER: (*Pointedly*) The haunted what?

HANSEL: (*Slowly*) The haunted castle.

FREIDA: (*to HANSEL*) You knew there was a castle and didn't care to mention it?!

HANSEL: I knew there was a *haunted* castle. I don't bring up haunted castles.

GUNTER: (*Grabbing HANSEL and pointing him towards RUBI and the BEAST*) Well you see those fine folks over there, Hansel? (*He nods.*) They are from that very UNhaunted castle, and travel to and fro on a very UNdangerous road. (*Picking him up by the shirt*) And I am very UNhappy about that (*GUNTER shoves Hansel*).

FREIDA: We can handle it, sir. Just one more path to pilfer!

LARS: (*Skipping around, singing to the tune of "Following the Leader"*) We'll go and rob the castle, the castle, the castle, cause pillaging the castle's the best thing that we know!

GUNTER: Stop that singing, you fool. (*HELMUT stops LARS.*) We'll have to come up with a plan so it doesn't seem obvious that the road has been cut off just after they came to town... (*THEY pull into a huddle and lights shift to RUBI and BEAST who have pulled DR.*)

RUBI: You still have the signet of your father?

BEAST: I doubt that my signet would matter.

RUBI: How could it not? If your father was a lord, surely you are.

BEAST: But a Lord of what kingdom? What year is it?

RUBI: 1768.

BEAST: (*Pales*) Are you sure?

RUBI: Yes; why?

BEAST: (*Sadly*) Rubi, my father died over a century ago.

RUBI: A century? (*He nods; she goes on, seriously.*) The Germanic Kingdoms have been overtaken, broken, and had a half a dozen rulers since then... (*In awe*) And you've been alone in the castle all that time? (*Tenderly*) How did this happen to you? (*He turns away.*)

BEAST: If you think the signet will help, you and this town are welcome to it. (*He turns back to her*) but I make you no promises, Rubi.

RUBI: You don't have to. (*Smiles, hopeful.*) No other castle or Lord is over this land, or Kleiner Weiler would have gone to them already. I'm sure the signet will at least get the letter to someone who matters at court. You can help, Stevard. If you'll try.

BEAST: I will on one condition.

RUBI: Which is?

BEAST: Call me by my name again, if you please.

RUBI: (*Nobly*) Stevard, you can help these people.

BEAST: (*Nods, then shrinks a little*) You tell them.

73

RUBI: (*Crosses Center and calls the attention of the town*) Friends! Stevard has informed me that his father was a Lord to the Hapsburgs, and he possesses a signet! (*Everyone cheers with surprise*).

SAFFI: So he will help us?

SMITH: (*Suspicious*) At what cost?

BEAST: (*Stepping forward*) No cost. It has been a long time since anyone claimed lordship over this land, so I don't know that my signet will make any difference at all.

RUBI: But we are willing to try, are we not?

BEAST: We are.

GLENA: Then so are we! What do we do?

RASMUS: We'll have to send trust of payment with the letter, to show that a regiment can be supported here.

RUBI: (*An idea strikes*) If everyone contributes the money they would have paid to clear the roads, I feel certain we will have enough. Bring it to the Ball! There, you can write the letter, Lord Sholtze will sign and seal it and we will send it on its way!

RASMUS: (*Grandly*) I will carry it safely to its delivery, I swear it!

GLENA: Agreed. Everyone else?

TOWN: Ja! (*Cheering*)

RUBI: In a fortnight, then! Auf wiedersehen.

> (*TOWN says goodbye.*)

> (*Lights dim, but focus on GUNTER watching RUBI and BEAST leave.*)

FREIDA: The nerve!

LARS: Soldiers! Here? Well, it was a good run, lads.

GUNTER: We're not leaving like this.

HELMUT: But, soldiers will be coming.

HANSEL: I don't like soldiers.

GUNTER: I don't like poverty! It's simple, you dolts. They've actually done us a favor.

FREIDA: How you figure?

GUNTER: Instead of bleeding the town dry over months, we'll take all they have in one night.

LARS: All they have?

GUNTER: Didn't you hear? They'll have all their guldens at the Masquerade next week. And everyone is invited.

    (Lights out.)

SCENE 4: THE CASTLE

(Curtain is closed; lights up front of curtain. There is a brick oven and a table where we see BEAST and RUBI baking, rolling out dough to make a Linzer Torte. They are smattered with flour, smears of butter, etc. BEAST is rolling out tiny snakes of dough for the lattice. BERGEN, LEDER, DOPPLE and GANGER come in and out as needed.)

BEAST: I still don't understand why such decorations are necessary. Bergen says he can do a lattice in strips.

RUBI: This is a Linzer Torte; I'd like to make as my mother did. Besides, it is more fun this way!

BEAST: Hmph. I thought you didn't like a mess.

RUBI: This is a meaningful mess. You like torte don't you?

BEAST: Fruit should not be cooked.

RUBI: (*Laughing*) Well, that may be why you don't see the value in it.

BEAST: Hmph.

LEDER: (*Coming between them*) No, roll it like this.

BERGEN: Too much jam!

RUBI: What did the two of you do without me?

DOPPLE: Cooked less!

GANGER: Played more.

BEAST: You certainly did.

RUBI: Now, now. There's no reason to be angry with them.

LEDER: First batch looks done, Rubi. (*RUBI goes to check the Linzer Auge—mini tortes—in the brick stove.*)

RUBI: Ooo! Golden and perfect!

BERGEN: They won't stay golden! Pull them out.

(RUBI Reaches in to pull the torte out.)

BEAST: (*Rushes in*) You'll burn yourself! (*RUBI stops; BERGEN and LEDER freeze, looking at the BEAST*) Let me. (*GNOME's mouths fall open. BEAST puts the torte on the table.*)

RUBI: Thank you.

BEAST: You're welcome. (*Awkward silence.*)

RUBI: (*Shrugs*) Who wants the first taste? (*BEAST shakes his head emphatically*) Then it is up to me. (*RUBI picks up an bite, blows to cool it then, SHE enjoys the taste very much, jumping up and down and making happy noises; takes another bite. RUBI offers the last bite to BEAST, who is surprised by the comfortable gesture. He takes the bite and enjoys it, too.*)

BEAST: Delicious!

RUBI: Thank you.

BEAST: (*Surprised*) I didn't mean it as a compliment.

RUBI: (*Laughs*) You gave words. I choose how to receive them.

BEAST: Hmph.

RUBI: Why are you in such a foul mood?

LEDER: As opposed to...?

RUBI: (*Playful reprimand*) Come now. He's been downright pleasant for weeks. But today...

BEAST: (*Down*) I should never have agreed to the Ball.

RUBI: Ah.

BEAST: (*Silent for a moment, toying with the dough.*) I won't go. You can be the hostess.

RUBI: (*Hands over the cooking to BERGEN and LEDER*) What is this really about?

BEAST: The ball is to please you. Everyone will have more fun if I am nowhere near.

RUBI: Weren't they all kind to you at the village?

BEAST: You are naïve, Rubi. If they knew, that this is what I am, that this is the curse I bear—they would run from me. I know it.

RUBI: I haven't.

BEAST: You would have if you could have. I remember your face the first time you looked at me.

RUBI: I had just left my family for eternal servitude, alone and scared. You were belittling and mean! (*BEAST hangs his head.*) But you are different, now (*comfortingly*).

BEAST: No. I am still a beast (*looking at his hands—looking at himself in a pot*).

RUBI: (*Proof*) You saved me from burning myself.

BEAST: So?

RUBI: The first month I was here, you actually threw rocks on me as you walked in the door. You didn't even notice! But that's not you anymore. You are far less a beast today than you were ten months ago. I don't find you frightful at all, now.

BEAST: (*Bigger*) You must not have taken a good look recently.

RUBI: (*Laughing*) Have you looked at me? (*Indicating the flour all over her.*)

BEAST: (*Like he's been caught*) No, of course not! Why would I? That's weird. I never look at you. Ever. I don't even know what color your hairs are.

RUBI: (*Laughing*) My what?

BEAST: Your hair. Or your eyes. Nothing.

RUBI: (*Moves closer to him*) Really? (*He continues to look somewhere else*) Would you like to know the color of my eyes?

BEAST: No.

RUBI: Oh. (*Turning the conversation*) Would it matter to you if my eyes were a certain color or other?

BEAST: (*Looking at her*) Of course not.

RUBI: What if my hair all fell out?

BEAST: (*Savvy*) I know why you are asking.

RUBI: You may know, but do you understand? You have so much to offer if you would stop worrying about what other people think! Just tell yourself "I am a hairy beast and everyone likes it!"

BEAST: (*Dryly*) That's ridiculous.

RUBI: So is hiding away in a castle, convinced that no one will ever like you.

BEAST: That's actually quite sensible if you are a beast.

RUBI: Pish-tosh. (*Sincerely*) I want you there. Is that enough?

BEAST: (*Grumbling but flattered*) I suppose so.

RUBI: Good; then it's settled: we will have a wonderful time tomorrow, you and I. And some other people, too, if they want. Now hand me that Torte for the oven.

SCENE 5: THE MASQUERADE

(Curtains open and lights up on the interior of the castle set for a party. A large Banquet table set upstage right with food and candles. A pedestal table is Center with flowers and an opaque fancy tablecloth. Benches around the edges of the room. VILLAGERS are dancing. After the first dance, WINDY who has been dancing clumsily, leaves her partner to join DIANA near EVENTYR.)

EVENTYR: I can't believe this is finally happening. What a glorious event!

WINDY: It's like a dream. I am at an actual party, dancing with actual people!

DIANA: Only because they don't know you actually aren't.

WINDY: Aren't what?

DIANA: People.

WINDY: (*Cross*) Oh, you spoil sport. Why do you have to bring that up at a time like this?

DIANA: (*Honestly*) I don't spoil sport. I'm the best at sports!

KNIGHTLY: (*Joining them*) Please stop bickering, ladies. (*Smiling at the room*) People are staring ...

WINDY: I'm a work of art, Knightly, they are staring at my beauty.

JESTER: No, that's not it. (*She glares at him*)

EVENTYR: Let her enjoy it, Jester. It's a special occasion, one we always hoped would come.

WIT: Speak for yourself. I enjoyed things as they were.

EVENTYR: (*Wistfully*) Ah yes, freedom to say whatever you want with no fear of consequence? Amusing certainly.

DIANA: Bah. A cowardly existence.

JESTER: Sticks and stones may break the bones–

WIT: But it's words that do the most damage.

DIANA: Tell that to my staff, Knot-head. (*Bops him on the nose and WIT cries out*).

EVENTYR: Diana, I understand why you are cross. We all feel it coming.

DIANA: (*Bravely*) I don't know what you mean.

WINDY: Yes you do. That feeling that something is about to...

KNIGHTLY: (*Anxious*) Stop talking about it, Windy. If we all feel it, then we certainly don't need to talk about it. (*To DIANA*) Shall we?

DIANA: Maybe in your better dreams.

> (*WINDY takes his arm and rushes across the room. MUSIC halts and RUBI enters SL staircase in a fantastic gown and mask.*)

RUBI: Welcome, everyone to the Masquerade Ball! There is plenty to eat and drink; enjoy yourselves!

(*EVERYONE cheers. RUBI continues down the stairs to join the group. GLENA finds her.*)

GLENA: *Gute Maske* Frauline!

RUBI: What a stunning costume! Who is it under the mask?

(GLENA *reveals her face.*)

RUBI: Glena! How splendid! Is everything ready?

GLENA: All but the signature, I think. Rasmus and Hedda wrote the thing. I just brought my gulden.

SMITH: So where is the lord of manor, Rubi?

RUBI: (*Looking around*) I was hoping he would be ready before me.

GLENA: (*Teasing*) So he could watch you come down those stairs?

CLARA: You were right to make a grand entrance, my dear, this gown is spectacular.

ANKA: Be sure to tell everyone it's one of ours.

RUBI: I'll shout it from the rooftops if that's what it takes. (*ANKA smiles, SMITH asks her for a dance. A group begins to assemble and RUBI is looking for BEAST, who appears from behind her wearing a mask that simply covers his eyes.*)

BEAST: Are you looking for someone?

RUBI: (*Smiles, but doesn't turn around*) Yes.

BEAST: Do you not see him in the assembly?

RUBI: (*Turning to look at him; he bows graciously, very old fashioned*) As it happens, I do see who I have been looking for. (*BEAST straightens.*)

FRITZ: Take your places!

> (*People choose partners and take their places in a circle.*)

BEAST: (*HE offers his paw to her*) Shall we? (*Sincerely*) I'll endeavor not to disappoint.

RUBI: You already exceed my expectations, sir. (*Laughs, fondly*) What have you done with my beast?

BEAST: (*Meaningfully*) I have tamed him for you.

(*HE leads her to their place. This dance should be loud and fun; a good chance for some folk dancing.*)

(*RASMUS and HEDDA enter.*)

RASMUS: The letter is ready, my lord! Prepared for your seal!

BEAST: Oh good. Rasmus, isn't it?

RASMUS: Yes, sir.

RUBI: I'll fetch a candle and sealing wax.

BEAST: Oh no, let me.

RUBI: Are you sure you can find it?

BEAST: (*Fond teasing*) Unless you put it somewhere where something has no business being.

RUBI: (*Knowingly*) Oh, so you *do* know where it is.

BEAST: I'll be right back.

GLENA: Tsk, Tsk, Tsk.

RUBI: What?

GLENA: Just a few days and you've got that lord in it deeper than a fat man in a quagmire.

RUBI: What on earth do you mean? (*GLENA gives her a look.*) Oh, please, Glena. Surely you don't think that—

GLENA: Your denial gives you away precious. You're in it, too.

RUBI: (*Proudly*) What if I am?

GLENA: Then I get to bake the cake.

RUBI: I'd say that's rather premature...

GLENA: I'll send away for the sugar.

RUBI: Glena!

CLARA: (*Breaking in*) Why do you need more sugar? What are we talking about?

RUBI: Nothing.

GLENA: Just that there may be bells ringing in this girl's future.

RUBI: (*To CLARA*) Tell her she is being ridiculous!

CLARA: Only because she is just barely ordering the sugar. I sent away for the lace when last you came to town.

RUBI: You what?!

> (*The doors to the castle burst open and in walks the BANDITS, led by GUNTER.*)

GUNTER: Ah, my friends! Here you all are! What a magnificent spread, what a wonderful gathering! (*Crossing to RUBI*) Thank you for the invitation, Frauline.

RUBI: (*Tense*) My pleasure, Herr... ?

GUNTER: Gunter Rask, at your service.

RUBI: (*Recognizing*) Gunter *Rask?* Aren't you a merchant in Hamburg?

GUNTER: (*Smug*) Well, I played one once. (*He removes his mask, and the other BANDITS who had been dancing as guests remove theirs as well.*)

RUBI: I know who you are! You lost my father's fortune.

GUNTER: Your father lost his own fortune.

RUBI: You baited him, though!

HELMUT: (*Breaking in*) And we robbed him in the wood!

LARS: Yeah, we left him for dead!

GUNTER: Shut up, you fools!

RUBI: (*Strongly*) You ruined my family.

GUNTER: Your father would have done it on his own in time, no doubt. I am not to blame for his misdeeds. Besides, you seem to have landed on your feet.

RUBI: (*Pointedly*) I am a servant here, working off my father's debt.

> (*The VILLAGE guests gasp.*)

GUNTER: (*Looking her up and down*) Oh I highly doubt that. Not in that get-up.

RUBI: It's a gift.

GUNTER: (*Calculating*) Really? (*Prying*) If you are the servant, where is the lord of the manor?

RASMUS: (*Scrambling for distraction*) He took the letter to the soldiers himself two days ago.

SMITH: (*Supporting the deception*) We decided it couldn't wait.

ANKA: This party is to welcome him back.

> (*RUBI smiles at their support.*)

FREIDA: Nice try. No one has left here in days!

HANSEL: Yeah, we been watchin' this place!

GUNTER: Like you watched the road to this castle for months? (*HANSEL nods emphatically*) I thought so. (*Pushes HANSEL*) Go search the castle. And start looting while you're at it! (*BANDITS exit.*)

SAFFI: There is no need to do anything rash.

GUNTER: I disagree. I had a fine plan in the making, you know. I was going to come by my gains honestly. Well, I was going to come by them peaceably.

EMIL: How?

GUNTER: I see a demand, and I supply a service. Of course, I also supplied the demand...

SAFFI: (*Realizing*) You lead the bandits that choke our town.

GLENA: (Furious) And you had the gall to extort us for protection!

GUNTER: (*Falsely apologetic*) You're right. That was bad of me. So underhanded. (*Places hand on his heart*) I vow to give up my conniving ways! I promise to be honest and straightforward; from this day on, no longer a man of false confidence. (*Pulls out a musket, pointing it at GLENA*) So hand over the guldens.

EMIL: But you just said...

GUNTER: I said I wasn't going to connive. I never said I'd give up robbing at musket-point. (*Cocks the musket*) The gulden, if you please. Every bit.

> (*VILLAGERS start depositing their gulden on the table and gathering DR in a group; LARS and HELMUT re-enter; with bags full of stolen riches; begin adding the gulden to a bag.*)

HEDDA: (*Whispering to RUBI*) What do we do?

SMITH: We can fight them. Half are off in the castle somewhere. I could take four by myself.

ANKA: (*Concerned*) You'll be hurt!

RUBI: (*Calming*) We mustn't rush headlong into danger.

ANKA: Rubi's right; gulden can be replaced, but handsome people cannot.

SMITH: (*Perking up*) What kind of people?

ANKA: (*Suddenly shy*) Just...people.

GLENA: (*Glaring at GUNTER and BANDITS*) I doubt we'd get hurt. Only weakness draws a gun and calls it power.

RUBI: (*Putting a hand on GLENA's shoulder*) Don't, Glena. Once he has the money, he'll leave. We can start again.

GUNTER: (*Shouting*) Stop your whispering or I'll have to separate you! In fact, Helmut, get the pretty one away from the other one. Bring her here. (*HELMUT grabs GLENA*) Not that one! I said the pretty one! (*HELMUT grabs SMITH; exasperated.*) Oh fine I'll do it! (*GUNTER crosses to RUBI and drags her to the chaise DL. VILLAGERS protest and he tosses RUBI to the chaise.*) You just sit there looking frightened so no one tries anything stupid. (*Looks at her*) Yes. Make that face, that's the face I mean.

> (*FREIDA and HANSEL enter with the BEAST between them.*)

FREIDA: Look who we found!

GUNTER: (*To RUBI*) This is the lord of the castle? I thought you said he was long gone. Tsk, Tsk, Tsk. And you're all up in arms because *I'm* a liar.

BEAST: What is going on here?

GUNTER: I already did this part. Basically, I'm here to take everything.

BEAST: From me?

GUNTER: I believe in equality! (*Smiling*) I steal from everyone.

BEAST: Please, just take my things. I'm sure it's more than enough to satisfy even one such as you. Leave the villagers be.

GUNTER: Private islands are expensive in the West Indies. I need all I can get.

BEAST: These people have worked hard for what they have.

GUNTER: I understand the philosophy. I just don't buy into it. I take what I want because I can. It works for me.

BEAST: Well it doesn't work for me.

GUNTER: Will it work for you if I threaten the precious neck of your fine lady? (*Picks up RUBI and threatens her with a knife.*)

BEAST: (*Threatening*) Don't. Touch. Her.

GUNTER: (*Disgusted*) Ugh. If you are going to be threatening, at least stay relevant. For instance; you could say "Stop touching her" or "Don't hurt her." (*Twists RUBI's arm and she screams*) Oh, too late for that one.

BEAST: (*Coldly*) I will tear you to shreds.

GUNTER: (*To the crowd*) Tough talk from the lord of the manor! (*Tosses RUBI to the chaise and goes to BEAST*) Let's take this mask off and see what kind of man you really are. (*Tries to rip off mask, finds it's his face. Yells.*) That's his face!

LARS: He's the monster!

> (*BEAST throws off HANSEL and FREIDA; the VILLAGERS gasp. GLENA looks to RUBI, who obviously knew all along.*)

HANSEL: I told you this place was cursed!

> (*FREIDA and HANSEL fall over themselves to get away. BEAST roars; GUNTER and BANDITS are chased off.*)

RUBI: We have to get all of the bandits in here together—trap them!

GLENA: Don't just stand there, Smith! Emil! Anka and Clara! Find a weapon and defend our town! To the Beast!

DIANA: (*Excited*) I've waited centuries for this!

KNIGHTLY: To the Master!

GNOMES: To the Master!

(VILLAGERS run out after the BANDITS chasing them through the castle to music. HANSEL enters from DSL crossing the stage to run up the stairs: WIT spits in his face, HANSEL screams and runs off DL. GUNTER and BANDITS enter USR, GUNTER motions for them to split up. Some exit USL to the Kitchen, others exit DR. DI-ANA enters, chasing GUNTER kicking him to the ground, attempting to hit him with the sword, hr rolls and pulls her down, exiting UR. DIANA goes to the stairs to wait for another chance. HEDDA, ALBERTA, ANKA enter CSR and hide under the pedestal table. GNOMES enter DSR and create speed bumps. RAS-MUS, & a VILLAGER run over the GNOMES followed by PIPO and a BANDIT. PIPO trips on the speed bumps and is dragged out by the other BANDIT. SMITH runs on from SR and tries to pull ANKA out from under the table. GUNTER runs on from USR and leaps over their joined hands, followed by the BEAST who leaps over the table. SMITH joins ANKA under the table. EMIL and SAFFI run on from SR and are met Center by HELMUT and JOHANNA. EMIL/SAFFI scream and run upstage around the table, chased by BANDITS, who are then tripped by HEDDA. HEDDA and ALBERTA chase JOHANNA offstage. SMITH pulls ANKA out from under the table and HELMUT grabs SMITH by the hand. ANKA and HELMUT tug SMITH back and forth until HELMUT wins. ANKA strides over and slaps HELMUT, causing her to spin and fall to the ground. SMITH, appreciatively, takes ANKA by the hand and runs off Left with her. GLENA chases a bunch of BAN-DITS across stage from UL to UR wielding a rolling pin.

FRIEDA and HANSEL enter from SL and hide under the pedestal table, the GNOMES pull them by their feet just far enough for GLENA and a VILLAGER to bop them on the heads with a ladle and rolling pin. GNOMES drag the BANDITS DR and DL. Both groups, BANDITS and VILLAGERS, come running down both sides of the staircase and crash together in the center where the stairs meet, falling in a huge jumble. SMITH enters R with PIPO on his back, EMIL removes PIPO and tosses him into the pile. All the VILLAGERS run off in different directions as RUBI takes EMIL to DC to scold him for getting into the battle without his mother. They are surrounded by bandits who advance. RUBI picks up EMIL and swings him around, kicking down all the bandits in a circle. RUBI and EMIL exit SL, followed by BANDITS. GUNTER enters SR followed by the BEAST and is caught under the arms by LARS and ANDERS, who carry him off SR, followed by everyone shouting. The BEAST braces for an attack, but everyone runs right past him and he is left Center stage, bewildered. RUBI sees him.)

RUBI: There you are! We have a plan—we're going to round them up then shoo them out like frightened birds.

BEAST: (*Shocked*) They are fighting *with* me?!

WINDY: (*Who has been standing near JESTER and WIT the whole time*) Well, some of us are biding our time.

RUBI: (*Taken aback*) Of course they are. What did you think was happening?

BEAST: I thought they were frightened and running from me.

RUBI: No! They are with you!

BEAST: (*Tenderly*) I thought maybe you were…

RUBI: What? Leaving? You threatened to tear a man apart for me.

BEAST: (*Sincerely*) I would have given him anything. I would have given him the magic of the castle if I could.

RUBI: (*She touches his face*) You big lug.

BEAST: (*Confused*) I don't know how to take that.

> (*RUBI kisses his paw.*)

BEAST: (*Tenderly*) Rubi…

GLENA: (*Shouting from offstage*) We've got you now, you filthy *Lumpenpack*!

> (*GUNTER charges onstage, BEAST pulls RUBI behind him and they stand back to back, ready to face the fight. GUNTER seizes his musket from the table and hits BEAST, taking RUBI as hostage. BANDITS move SL and VILLAGERS stay SR, concerned for RUBI. GUNTER backs RUBI up the stairs towards the door.*)

> (*RUBI sees KNIGHTLY and DIANA perched on the stairs, laughs.*)

GUNTER: Why are you laughing? You are at my mercy. I'll kill you, you know!

WIT: You know what mister? (*GUNTER turns to see the face on the wall, utterly shocked*)

JESTER: You talk too much.

> (*DIANA disarms GUNTER and KNIGHTLY kicks him downstage into BEAST. WINDY pulls RUBI to safety as BEAST throws GUNTER further DL towards the fireplace, in full animal mode. RUBI breaks away from WINDY.*)

RUBI: Stevard! This isn't you anymore!

BEAST: (*Panting over GUNTER, controlling himself*) I will spare you and your band if you leave now.

>   (*GUNTER nods, appearing terrified, and rises to leave. RUBI rushes to BEAST and GUNTER pulls KNIGHTLY's sword, swinging in an attack at BEAST who rolls out of the way.*)

DIANA: (*Tossing BEAST her sword*) Master!

>   (*GUNTER and BEAST engage in a swordfight that roams all over the stage, moving VILLAGERS as needed. It ends with BEAST coming down on GUNTER who is bent back over the pedestal table until he is disarmed and begging, truly frightened for his life.*)

BEAST: You have found mercy here. Leave and never return.

>   (*FREIDA and LARS carry out GUNTER before he has a chance to try anything else stupid.*)

GOOSEY: And stay out!

>   (*VILLAGERS and CASTLE cheer and surround BEAST and RUBI in a big group hug. RUBI roars playfully and BEAST roars back. EVERYONE stops and takes one big step away from RUBI and BEAST, awkward.*)

HEDDA: (*Touching WINDY*) This castle is truly magical.

WINDY: (*Giggles*) Thank you.

GLENA: How did this happen?

SMITH: I can't believe it!

EMIL: (*Innocently*) You really are a monster.

>   (*Silence.*)

RUBI: Actually, Emil, it depends on your definition.

CLARA: He certainly doesn't act like a monster.

RUBI: He can hear you, you know.

CLARA: I'm sorry.

GLENA: I'm not. (*Crossing to BEAST*) I owe you quite a debt, my lord. I've not heard of a person in your position willing to fight tooth and nail for his people. I'm truly grateful to be under your honest and kind stewardship. (*Curtsey.*)

SMITH: And I! (*Bows.*)

HEDDA and SAFFI: And I! (*Curtsey.*)

ALL: Ja, Ja! To the Beast!

EMIL: (*Childlike, taking BEAST by the paw*) Can we use the magic again, to protect the village if they come back?

BEAST: (*Touched*) I would gladly offer the magic of the castle, but I don't control it. I don't even know how it came to be here. We will send for the soldiers as planned. I will stand with each of you come what may! I will help you rebuild the village—using the stones of this very castle if necessary!

ALL: Ja, Ja!

RUBI: (*Laughing*) When you tear down this castle, then where will we live?

BEAST: In a modest house near the town.

RUBI: Alone?

BEAST: (*Smiling*) That wasn't my plan...

RUBI: I'm sure I can care for a modest home, my lord.

BEAST: We would do it together, Rubi. If you'll have me. (*She is silent; he goes on, earnestly.*) I *like* working alongside you. You make

93

everything more fun, more beautiful. Even me. I love the world when I see it with you. So, will you? (drops to one knee) Will you marry me?

> (RUBI nods emphatically, too overcome to speak, and kisses BEAST.)

CLARA: Good thing I ordered the lace.

GLENA: We'll have a proper party then, none of this thievery and fighting to ruin the day!

> (ALL cheer.)

SAFFI: In the center of town!

> (ALL cheer.)

RASMUS: That is, if this is a public event, your lordship.

BEAST: (*Beaming, with RUBI under his arm.*) Of course! Everyone is invited! The entire country may attend! Tourists from everywhere to see this great beauty wed her beast!

RUBI: (*Laughing*) Now we are an attraction?!

BEAST: You want to help the town, don't you?

RUBI: Aren't you concerned what others will think?

BEAST: I think well of me, and you love me. No one else's opinion matters.

> (The CASTLE pieces move back to original places as dialogue continues.)

GLENA: *Wie wahr!* (so true)

BEAST: (*Raising a glass for a toast. VILLAGERS follow.*) To our future! (*BEAST becomes dizzy and weak before he drinks, backing up, falling onto and flipping over the table.*)

> (EVERYONE react as music swells and lights change.)

RUBI: Goosey! What is happening to him?! Knightly! WINDY?! (*CASTLE are frozen and unmoving.*) Someone help him!

> (*EVENTYR exits the painting with smoke, lights and music change.*)

RUBI: (*Confused*) Eventyr? Can you help him?

EVENTYR: (*Heavily*) Rubi Smuk. He is beyond the help that I am able to give.

RUBI: (*In tears*) He cannot be dead.

EVENTYR: (*Conversationally*) Oh, no—that's not what I meant. Sorry. He will wake soon.

RUBI: Did you do this?

EVENTYR: His father made the choice and I performed the magic.

EMIL: Aha! Magic, mother! I told you.

SAFFI: Yes, dear, you knew all along.

RUBI: I thought the magic was just for the castle. What does this have to do with Stevard?

EVENTYR: His father, a simple tenant in this land found me injured in the woods centuries ago. As I was in his debt I was required to grant him a wish. Silas wished to have all the riches and power of a king without ever having to work for it.

SAFFI: (*Sarcastically*) Sounds reasonable.

EVENTYR: (*Not catching the sarcasm*) The wish had to be balanced. A child reflecting on the outside what such a selfish wish created on the inside. It was supposed to change his mind. Instead, he found a way to imprison me and extract all of my magic to care for the castle. I had to break myself into little pieces to do all that had to be done.

RUBI: But what about Goosey, Knightly? Diana? They were—

EVENTYR: Fragments of *me* scattered through the castle.

RUBI: They are gone?

EVENTYR: (*Smiling, loving*) They are still here. They were an extension of me. They are all me!

RUBI: (*Doubtful*) Even Jester and Wit?

EVENTYR: Especially Jester and Wit. Saying whatever I want is one aspect I will miss.

RUBI: (*Sadly*) They were my friends.

EVENTYR: We still are. *(RUBI and EVENTYR embrace; RUBI looks to STEVARD)* Silas punished Stevard far worse than the spell intended. He saw Stevard as a constant reminder that he could not provide for himself or his family.

CLARA: That must have been awful.

HEDDA: For them both.

EVENTYR: His mother did her best to teach Stevard that he was not responsible for his father's anger.

RUBI: (*Understanding*) That's why she downplayed beauty and kindness and grace. To ease his pain.

EVENTYR: She didn't believe he was capable of it, so she pretended they weren't worthwhile virtues.

SMITH: Damned stupid.

ANKA: Smith!

SMITH: Well it was. Even I know that without hope of achieving beauty, there's no point even picking up a hammer.

RASMUS: *Sehr Wahr!*

RUBI: This explains so much. His loneliness, his entitlement.

GLENA: All lords are like that.

RUBI: You weren't here. I've never seen such a contradictory person. He was kind enough to spare my father, but cruel and temperamental over the smallest things, yet curious and—young. He was so young. (*Thinking of his pain, RUBI cries*)

EVENTYR: He doesn't need those tears now. He made the choice his father never could. Don't you see! He is victorious! He broke the spell.

RUBI: (*Hopeful*) My Beast?

EVENTYR: Gone. But the one you love remains.

> (*STEVARD stands, a little dizzy, and looks to both EVENTYR and RUBI.*)

STEVARD: What happened? Why am I—?

> (*EVERYONE looks at STEVARD, marveling and moved. He is uncomfortable and crosses to RUBI.*)

STEVARD: Please tell me what's going on. I feel strange.

RUBI: Long story short—(*looks to EVENTYR who shrugs and nods*) Um, remember when you said you tamed the beast for me?

STEVARD: Yes.

RUBI: (*Emotional, happy*) You were right. (*She takes his hands and holds them up for him to see.*)

STEVARD: (*Laughs; runs to the banquet table and checks his reflection in a dish, marvels at his appearance*) I'm a man! Look at me! I'm normal! I'm handsome!! (*Whoops and shouts—celebrates*) I'm a handsome man! (*HE turns to RUBI who has been laughing at the display*) Do you like it?

RUBI: To be honest, your face wasn't your charm to begin with.

STEVARD: (*Sincerely*) Thank you.

RUBI: (*Smiling*) What makes you so sure I meant that as a compliment?

STEVARD: (*Flirting*) You think I'm charming.

RUBI: (*Sincerely*) Oh yes I do.

STEVARD: And human.

RUBI: And kind.

STEVARD: And handsome?

RUBI: (*Nods, loving*) And *beautiful*. (*They giggle.*)

GLENA: Alright, you two. Break it up.

STEVARD: Nein! (*Dips RUBI and kisses her, everyone whoops*) This is a celebration! Fritz! Play the music and let us dance!

> (*They Dance.*)

> (*Lights out.*)

END

Made in the USA
Monee, IL
09 August 2021